Enjoy the Old Testament with me.

By June Little

©Copyright June Little 2015 **ISBN 978-1-326-45465-4**
All rights reserved. No part of this publication may be reproduced, stored in a retrieval system, or transmitted, in any form or by any means, electronic, mechanical photocopying, recording, or otherwise, without the written prior permission of author.
This book is printed by LULU (on demand printing).
Contact for any enquiries to author.
June Little,27, Newfield Rd, Newhaven, East . Sussex, BN9 9ND.
Tel: 07871181958
Also available as e-book

Text formatting annotation

All Holy Bible verses taken from the NIV (UK) edition. The formatting on this edition is kept in this book style. Note when God is mentioned as 'he, him, me, my etc it is kept lower case. Narrative text by author is in these instances are in capitals.

Foreword

'Sometimes it is like doing a puzzle trying to put together the different stories of the Old Testament and we are often left with gaps. This is a wonderful contextualisation of the Old Testament stories and explanation of God's purposes and plans not just for his people then but us today. June writes from a wealth of deep knowledge and years of study of her subject.

I highly recommend this book to someone who is a new follower of Jesus to provide a firm basis for their understanding of the bible as well as for more mature believers who want a better understanding of the pattern of scripture. '

Jackie Harland
Pastor CityCoast Church Portslade Sussex

Acknowledgement

This book would probably never have come into existence if it were not for the prophetic words of my pastor Jacky Harland who declared that I had a book in me and though I allowed several years to pass before I acted upon her words, it has at last come to fruition ; thank you Jackie for your encouragement.

I also would like to acknowledge the influence that David Pawson's "Unlocking the Bible" has had on me. I have learnt so much from the pages of that book which has stood me in good stead in my teaching of the Bible.

Lastly I owe a great debt to my busy daughter Ellen Cranton who has carefully typed up my handwritten pages and to my dear friend, Susan Hill, who has spent much time going through my manuscript, tidying it up, designing the cover and preparing it for publication.

June Little 2015

Contents

Foreward	
Acknowledgement	
Introduction	
Genesis	1
Exodus	9
Leviticus	20
Numbers.	25
Deuteronomy	28
Joshua	31
Judges	35
Ruth	37
1 Samuel	39
2 Samuel	50
1 - 2 Kings	55
1 Chronicles	67
2 Chronicles	73
Ezra	83
Nehemiah	88
Esther	92
Job	97
Psalms	103
Proverbs	108
Ecclesiastes	110
Song of Solomon	116

Isaiah	118
Jeremiah	136
Lamentations	141
Ezekiel	144
Daniel	150
Hosea	156
Joel	159
Amos	162
Obadiah	164
Jonah	166
Micah	168
Nahum	171
Habakkuk	173
Zephaniah	176
Haggai	178
Zechariah	180
Malachi	183

Introduction

Why have I bothered to write a book about the contents of the thirty nine books which make up the Old Testament? Firstly because I feel an understanding of these books as a whole, not just certain well known passages, gives a far deeper appreciation of the New Testament.

Secondly I believe the Godhead, father, Son and Holy Spirit are "the same yesterday, today and forever" Heb.13.8 and therefore it is important to know what there is to know of them from the beginning of time as we know it.

When I became a Christian as a student the only available version of the Bible was the King James Bible, known to us as the Authorized Version. This version was hard to read, and make sense of, especially the Old Testament.

However when I took up my first teaching post, I was asked by my headmaster to fill in the gaps in my teaching timetable with a few lessons of Religious Education (R.E.) He was indifferent as to whether I had any knowledge of the subject - just keep the class quiet for thirty five minutes! I recognised this as a challenge to my young faith and was determined to do more than the headmaster had suggested. Hence my enrolment in evening classes at London Bible College.

At the time this was an hours train journey from my school. During my twice weekly visits there over a period of three years I acquired a very good grounding in both Old and New Testaments, plus a real love for the subject. I was well taught, I must have been to have stayed awake for two hours of lectures after a hectic day grappling with my first years of teaching.

It is that love of the Bible which has now so many excellent modern translations, that I desire to pass on to fellow Christians and to all who have an interest in what the Old Testament has to say.

I have been stirred on to do this partly because of the prejudice that I have encountered during my teaching years. I still teach a Bible group, even though I retired from school teaching over twenty years ago. I have been asked why I bothered so much with the Old Testament as the New was so much more important. It has been my practice to give each testament equal time and certainly my present group have appreciated this, as it has helped them to relate one testament to the other.

Many people have expressed the opinion that the God in the O.T has a different character from that of the God in the N.T. They would say that the God of the O.T is a God bent upon justice - ready to punish if His commandments are not kept. Whereas the God of the N.T is a God of love, ready to forgive and encourage. I beg to differ and have sought to emphasize in my teaching that there is only one God whose character has not changed; who is as loving in the O.T as He is in the N.T. He is also as just, meting out justice in the N.T as He did in the O.T.

Ever since the fall of mankind in the garden of Eden, God had a plan to bring us back to Himself by giving us the ultimate sacrifice of His Son, Jesus Christ. The personal acceptance of this sacrifice for the forgiveness of sins committed and to be committed is the most important step we can take for it gives a way forward to each of us to have a relationship with our heavenly Father, both Jew and Gentile. However before that could take place, God had to show us that we needed a Saviour.

He did this by choosing one man, Abraham with whom He forged a relationship by making promises to him which were implemented through the trust and obedience of Abraham and were passed on to all his descendants, who became the Israelites. This nation was the means through whom God's plan of redemption could take shape. In almost every book of the O.T there are clues, mainly in prophecy, which point forward to the time when this Messiah or Christ would come to save His people.

As we follow the history of this Israelite nation we have revealed the way of life which pleases their God and what does not. They were no better or worse than the nations living around them, so God gave them His laws to live by and made certain these were passed on from one generation to the next. These laws were not easy to keep, for they like us had a tempter who sought to lead them astray. There was help at hand. When a law was broken, an animal sacrifice could be brought to the priest who would offer it up on the altar to obtain forgiveness for their wrong doing. This lasted until the next sin when a new sacrifice was needed.

God led His people out of slavery in Egypt and, through forty years of training in the wilderness provided all their needs. In return He expected their love, faithfulness and obedience. In the O.T we read how this chosen people blew hot and cold in their relationship with their God. When they took to doing their own thing and ignored God's ways they were given many warnings before punishment was meted out to knock them back into shape. It was to teach them and us of our need for a permanent Saviour - the animal sacrifice did not suffice. We might think we can approach God through our own righteousness but the history of the Israelites shows us otherwise!

When my granddaughters were very young, one Christmas morning I peeped into their bedroom to see how they were doing with their sack of presents, only to find their sacks untouched and the two girls busy in discussion. I joined them and was at once asked,

"Adam and Eve were the first people on earth, weren't they?" I agreed.

Mary and Joseph were the next people? Puzzled I replied no, and explained the lapse of thousands of years between the two events. "Why, since Jesus came to forgive sins did God not send Him down immediately sin came on earth?" "Did God not know of Adam and Eve's sin?"

I assured them He did and tried to give a simple answer to their very complex question, which seemed to suggest we could do without the O.T

Even the nation that God had specially trained, failed to live the holy life that He had demanded of them. When they were humble enough to realize their moral weakness God had the answer for them in the person of Jesus Christ, His Son Who gave us a new Covenant or Testament between us and our God.

In my book I am seeking to demonstrate that God did try to give mankind the chance to live His way by following His laws, but this was unsuccessful.

We cannot please God without the help of a Saviour!

Enjoy the Old Testament with me.

June Little 2015

Genesis

Genesis is the book of beginnings; the creation of our world. The first chapter states simply but profoundly how God tackled the task of creation and His judgement of each day's work as being good – perfectly complete. When He creates man in His own image His verdict is 'very good'.

He was on a different level from the rest of creation more complex in structure and given a free will. The conditions under which Adam and his helpmate Eve lived and worked were ideal and God was their friend who fellowshipped with them. They had complete freedom to enjoy all that was around them except for one tree, the tree of the knowledge of good and evil whose fruit they were forbidden to eat. This was the one and only law on which they could exercise their free will as to whether they chose to be obedient or not.

Satan in the guise of a serpent sought to query this law, targeting Eve so that she doubted the truth of what God said. He then caused her to desire the fruit and deceived her into believing that only good would come from the eating of it. Adam also was deceived into tasting the fruit which Eve offered him.

God, already knowing of their disobedience, knew that their wrong choice had allowed Satan to have a hold over them. If they were to eat of the fruit of the tree of everlasting life, also in the garden, Satan's domination would be forever; there would be no escape.

It was for their good that God removed them from the garden and warned them that their sinful act had caused their bodies to have a limited time on earth before they died.

However, God already had a plan for mankind to

escape the domination of Satan, which He spoke out to Satan,

"And I will put enmity between you and the woman, and between your offspring and hers; he will crush your head, and you will strike his heel."(Genesis 3:15).

A prophecy which referred to the coming of Jesus, the Son of God, but who came to earth as the seed of a woman, and died as the perfect sacrifice for mankind, went to hell and there dealt with Satan, wrestling from him his power over mankind.

Though Adam and Eve lost so much through this act of disobedience, and life indeed was hard for them outside of the garden, God's loving concern was still operating. They had realized they were no longer clothed in the glory of God and had sought to cover their nakedness with fig leaves – not very adequately. God made them garments out of animal skins, hence the first sacrifice made on their behalf.

God cannot look on sin; it is a barrier between Him and man but always God has made a way of escape. His plan through sacrifice, He gave careful instructions as to how this was to be done – the killing of a perfect animal on behalf of the sinful man. Cain, Adam's son, got this wrong by offering to God the produce he had grown, though his brother Abel understood the need to bring an animal. Cain was furious that his brother's offering was accepted and not his.

God spoke to him concerning his mistake and gave him the opportunity to put it right, pointing out that his attitude would allow Satan to have control of him. He refused to change and so ended up becoming the first murderer. He, too, became an outcast, but, God gave him a mark, so that no one took his life in revenge.

Genesis

We see in the following chapters of Genesis how sin takes a hold of mankind, passed down in the genes as one generation after another set their will against God. It is said of one man, Enoch that he walked with God, in a very wicked world, so that God rescued him by taking him to be with Himself before dying.

Such a universal wickedness had to be punished, but still God gave them a chance to return to Him. Before his rapture, Enoch had a son whom he named Methuselah, meaning 'when he dies, it will happen.' He was the longest living man; God gave the world 969 years before His judgement came upon them!

It was Methuselah's grandson Noah who walked in his grandfather's footsteps and heard from God at a time when the earth was corrupt in God's sight and was full of violence

'So God said to Noah, "I am going to put an end to all people, for the earth is filled with violence because of them." (Genesis 6:13).

Noah was given very detailed instructions on how to build a boat, large enough to hold his family plus two of every living beast, insect and bird.

Despite the warning, Noah's generation had no time for him or his boat, so that only Noah his wife, three sons and their wives – eight people in all, entered the boat with the animals plus provisions for all of them, a week before God flooded the land and destroyed every living thing on it except for those who chose the safety of the ark. Noah and his family who were attentive to God and offered up right sacrifices were well cared for after the flood.

Genesis

God made a covenant with Noah; this is a sacred promise between God and man which was for all generations to come.

"I have set my rainbow in the clouds and it will be the sign of the covenant between me and the earth …Never again will the waters become a flood to destroy all life." (Genesis 9:13,15).

Later when the generations which sprung from Noah's offspring became too full of themselves and sought to build a tower to reach up into the sky, God said that their unity of action came from their universal language.

He decided to scatter them by confusing their language so that they did not understand one another, thus preventing further exploits of this nature. As the world grew numerically, God decided to establish one nation close to himself whom He could instruct and they were to take His teachings into the rest of the world.

Abram, a Hebrew, was chosen to father this special nation; a man who heard from God and showed his faith in God by acting upon God's instructions to him to leave home with his wife to journey to a land where God would make him a great nation.

The promise was blessing….

"I will make you into a great nation, and I will bless you; I will make your name great, and you will be a blessing. I will bless those who bless you, and whoever curses you I will curse; and all peoples on earth will be blessed through you." (Genesis 12:2-3)

Genesis

This was the empowering promise from which Abram's faith grew.

God's love to him was not because of his perfection – he was still a sinful man who makes silly mistakes, but, he did listen to God and was obedient because he trusted God and believed Him and God counted his faith for righteousness. In fact he was known as the father of faith

'without faith it is impossible to please God' (Hebrews 11:6).

As the years passed by Abram did question whether he had heard God alright concerning his son, especially as his wife Sarah was passed childbearing years and indeed tried to help in this matter without God's say-so, but, that of his wife's. This plan went horribly wrong as God was not in it.

However, a few years later, God renewed His covenant with him saying

"As for me, this is my covenant with you: You will be the father of many nations. No longer will you be called Abram; your name will be Abraham, for I have made you a father of many nations. I will make you very fruitful; I will make nations of you, and kings will come from you."(Genesis 17:4-6).

It is very obvious that these special promises which God gave to Abraham were not just for his family, or even his nation, but, were a means for God to reach out to the whole earth; with the promises of land and riches came many responsibilities.

God did shower His love upon Abraham's descendants, but, He did expect them to use their free will to love and honour

Genesis

Him in return. God was true to His word and the son of promise, Isaac, was born to Abraham and Sarah when Abraham was 100 years old. He was circumcised when eight days old as God had instructed Abraham; a ritual that Abraham and all his male descendants were to undertake as a sign that they were special to God.

As we read through Genesis we see how this 'special' family developed; they were indeed very fruitful as God promised. We are never allowed to forget that though 'special' they were Adam's seed and as such, sin was in their genes. The family story encompasses Isaac the son and rightful heir of Abraham and the 'cast out' son Ishmael. Family disputes continued to Abrahams grandson Jacob and his brother Esau. Sin and strife went down the generations

When confronted with the wickedness of the people of Sodom, God was willing to listen to Abraham's plea that the city be saved if fifty righteous people be found in it which God agreed.

'Then Abraham approached him and said: "Will you sweep away the righteous with the wicked? What if there are fifty righteous people in the city? Will you really sweep it away and not spare the place for the sake of the fifty righteous people in it? "(Genesis 18: 23-24)

This number was whittled down to ten and eventually as these could not be found, the one righteous family were helped to escape before the place was destroyed. God has no desire to punish anyone who has faith in Him, but, there comes a time when evil has to be punished.

The story of Joseph, (Genesis 37 and 39 - 44) the great grandson of Abraham, is a clear example of God's love being victorious, despite the wickedness of his brothers, whose jealousy of their younger brother caused him great hardship. Joseph was a young man who listened to and heard God so that he received a powerful dream which suggested that he was to be in leadership over his brothers, and parents too. This really upset the family and when the opportunity arose the brothers got rid of him by selling him off to traders who took him into Egypt where he became a slave to Potiphar, an officer of Pharaoh.

Joseph continued to listen to God who caused him to find favour with his owner so that in due course he was given a great deal of responsibility within the home. However, Potiphar's wife fancied him and tried to persuade him to lie with her. When Joseph refused, she angrily wrenched at his garment and he made his escape, naked. She denounced him to her husband, and poor Joseph landed up in prison.

Again, Joseph kept close to God, who helped him give of his best, so that here too he was given responsibilities and was able to use God's wisdom in the interpretation of the dreams of two fellow inmates; his predictions proved true and Pharaoh's butler was restored to his former position.

Sometime later Pharaoh had dreams which his magicians were unable to interpret; the butler remembered his prison experience and the part Joseph played and recommended him to Pharaoh. Joseph was duly called, told the dreams and was able to explain to Pharaoh that there was to be seven years of plenty followed by seven years of famine. Joseph acknowledged that it was God who had given him the power of interpretation and the wisdom to know how best to prepare for the famine. Joseph was given the position and authority to put his plan into action.

Meanwhile his father and brothers in Canaan were also suffering the famine which Joseph had predicted, but, hadn't the same resources to deal with it and eventually their stockpile began to become so low that his father felt to send his older boys to Egypt to buy new supplies.Joseph meets up with his brothers, but on the first occasion doesn't reveal his identity as he wants them to return with their youngest brother who had been the closest to Joseph.

After time these supplies were gone and it was imperative for them to make a return journey, but knew supplies would only be given if the youngest son came too. Most reluctantly the father agreed and once again they came before Joseph who on this occasion revealed himself to them. Joseph was so happy to be restored to his family, but knew they would have mixed feelings because of their treatment of him. He helps them over this by saying;

"And now, do not be distressed and do not be angry with yourselves for selling me here, because it was to save lives that God sent me ahead of you." (Genesis 45:5).

The brothers return home with plentiful provisions to meet their needs whilst they pack up their families and belongings to move to Egypt with their aged father who is eager to meet his long lost son. Pharaoh had happily welcomed Joseph's family all seventy of them and given them a piece of land on which they could set up home and continue to earn a living as cattle and sheep farmers.

Exodus

Their story continues in the second book of the Bible, Exodus. There is a 400 year gap between the end of Genesis and the 1st Chapter of Exodus, during which time the small group of wealthy farmers had been very fruitful and multiplied to become over two million in number, but had also become slaves to the Egyptians to whom they had become such a threat numerically that the present Pharaoh ordered that all baby boys were to be thrown into the Nile at birth. Moreover the wickedness of the peoples who inhabited the land of Canaan had grown at such a rate that it needed to be stopped; God's justice was certainly due.

One baby boy who survived being in the Nile, having being rescued by Pharaoh's daughter, was Moses. He was taken to the royal palace and given the best education possible at the time; especially as he also had his Hebrew mother as his nurse who would school him in the ways of his own people, so that he was never ignorant of whom he truly was.

Thus when a young man he saw an Egyptian beat up a Hebrew slave and seeking to defend him, he slew the Egyptian. He became a marked man so had to flee for his life and for the next 40 years became a nomadic shepherd in the desert. Here he married a local woman, lived with her family and had two sons.

Whilst in the desert God drew Moses' attention to Him by means of a burning bush which the flames did not affect. As he approached this miracle God spoke, telling him to remove his shoes as he was on holy ground. It was here that God told him that he, Moses, was God's chosen leader to take

Exodus

the Hebrew people out of Egypt into the Promised Land.

Moses was horrified at the thought of such a call and made many excuses as to why he was not the man for the job. He felt utterly inadequate, incompetent and ignorant, but this did not deter God who assured him that He would provide the power and wisdom needed. When Moses spoke of his stutter which surely would prevent him speaking as a leader, God said that his brother Aaron would come alongside him and speak the words God gave him, to the people.

Moses then inquired as to what name he should give for God to the people. God gave him 'YHWH' no vowels so that the name could not be spoken in an offhand manner. It signified God's eternity without beginning or ending taken from the Hebrew verb "to be" and can be translated -He was, He is and He will be.-This personal name for God had many second names too, such as my provider, my helper, my protector, my healer. All of these were given to reveal God's character to His people and strengthen their faith in Him.

Moses did meet up with his brother Aaron on the way to Egypt with his family. During the journey God reminded Moses that he needed to circumcise his two sons as a sign that they belonged to the Hebrew people or Israelites after the name God gave Jacob (the father of Joseph)

Together Moses and his brother approached Pharaoh, having first spoken to the elders of the Israelites about God's plan for their departure from Egypt to a land, known to them as "the promised land" flowing with milk and honey. The Israelites were moved by the assurance that God cared for them and were ready to worship Him. However, Pharaoh's reaction to the plea of Moses and Aaron to let their people go into the desert to worship their God, was very negative.

Exodus

'Pharaoh said, "Who is the L*ORD*, *that I should obey him and let Israel go? I do not know the* L*ORD and I will not let Israel go." (Exodus 5:2)*

Their slave labour on the building sites making bricks was important to his projects; He hardened his heart and made life more difficult for the slaves by refusing straw for the bricks, thus making the bricks much heavier and their work harder – no time to have visions of escape.

That same day Pharaoh gave this order to the slave drivers and overseers in charge of the people: "You are no longer to supply the people with straw for making bricks; let them go and gather their own straw. But require them to make the same number of bricks as before; don't reduce the quota. They are lazy; that is why they are crying out, 'Let us go and sacrifice to our God." (Exodus 5:6-8)

Moses could not understand why God was allowing this and questioned it before God. However, God was aware of Pharaoh's opposition to His plan and replied to Moses,

"Now you will see what I will do to Pharaoh. Because of My mighty hand he will let them go; because of my mighty hand he will drive them out of his country". (Exodus 6:1)

'God also said to Moses, "I am the L*ORD, and I will bring you out from under the yoke of the Egyptians ------ and I will bring you to the land I swore with uplifted hand to give to Abraham, to Isaac and to Jacob. I will give it to you as a possession. I am the* L*ORD." (Exodus 6:6-8)*

This promise from God was not very well received by the people who were so bowed down by their cruel bondage. Even Moses felt that if he was getting nowhere with the people, how could he expect Pharaoh to listen to him.

Exodus

God asked him to go again to Pharaoh to request the people's release into the desert. Pharaoh wanted evidence from them that their God was more powerful than his, so he demanded a miracle of them. Aaron threw down his staff, as God commanded him, and it became a snake. Pharaoh summoned his magicians and they did the same thing by their secret arts, but, Aaron's staff swallowed up their staffs. Still Pharaoh's heart was hardened, so that he would not listen to them.

There followed a series of plagues which God sent upon the Egyptians one at a time, as a warning of God's displeasure with them. Each of the plagues was connected with a god they worshipped.

When the suffering was too much Pharaoh called for Moses to ask his God to take away the plague and he would let the people go.

God gave Pharaoh an opportunity to accept His request throughout until the last three plagues when God knew that Pharaoh's attitude would not change and so hardened his heart for him.

'But when Pharaoh saw that there was relief, he hardened his heart and would not listen to Moses and Aaron, just as the LORD had said.' (Exodus 8-15)

God told Moses to prepare the people for flight by first asking their neighbours for articles of silver and gold which they gladly gave in order to placate the Israelite God. God gave strict instructions to Moses concerning their escape which included the final plague, the death of the first born both animal and human. The Israelites were told to put the blood of the lamb killed for their final meal in Egypt on their doors to be seen by the angel of death who would then pass over them, and they were able to escape whilst the Egyptians were mourning their dead.

Pharaoh made one more attempt to retrieve his slaves, but God opened up the Red Sea for them to walk across on dry ground, but closed it when the Egyptian army came in hot pursuit. The Israelites had seen all the miracle plagues God had brought upon the Egyptians to cause the Pharaoh to let them go and yet needed to have much more assurance that God's concern for His people was demonstrated in His omnipotence.

God set physical laws for His creation, but He Himself was above such laws. They had thought God had brought them out in the desert to kill them when confronted with the sea before them and the Egyptian army behind

'Moses answered the people, "Do not be afraid. Stand firm and you will see the deliverance the LORD will bring you today. The Egyptians you see today you will never see again. The LORD will fight for you; you need only to be still." (Exodus 14:13-14)

Throughout the forty year journey through the wilderness, God was showing this people, with the mentality of slaves, that He was a Father God, who could be trusted when they put their faith in Him. Why did it take so long for them to make it to the 'promised land'? They were being fashioned into a nation who would move in unity under a godly leader, not a number of tribes wanting to do their own thing. Time and again they grumbled at Moses for not providing a satisfying diet and wanted to return to Egypt for a greater variety of vegetables.

When Moses laid their needs before the Lord, He responded with quails for meat and manna for bread. Water

Exodus

was also provided when requested or bitter water through a miracle made sweet. One of the most amazing miracles was the fact that their clothing and sandals remained usable for the whole time, despite the rough terrain over which they trailed. Each time they settled camp or moved on it was at the Lord's direction. When they had had three months in the wilderness, time to reflect on how God had freed them from slavery and provided for all their needs, God called Moses apart to meet Him up Mount Sinai to give him laws by which the Israelites were to live.

Their freedom was not dependent on this legislation that came about because they believed what Moses said God would do for them and followed this through by following the instruction on how they were to escape.

True their faith was often weak and they grumbled before thinking of going to God with their needs, but Moses intervened for them and as I have said, needs were met. However, with the legislation that Moses brought on stone tablets to them came a new contract or covenant.

If they would seek to live by the laws God put before them, then they would live in God's blessing. Every need would be provided, including good health; they would not suffer the diseases which nations around them were prone to. They would be fruitful and multiply as would their cattle. Should they choose to turn their backs on God's law, then they would suffer the curses which were the lot of ungodly nations.

There was provision for forgiveness when they did wrong, in the offering of a perfect clean animal. God's laws were introduced to give them a way of life which would set them apart from other nations. There was great satisfaction and joy in the keeping of them as the psalmist said,

Exodus

"I rejoice in following your statutes as one rejoices in great riches. I meditate on your precepts and consider your ways. I delight in your decrees; I will not neglect your word." (Psalms 119:14-16)

Whilst Moses was up Mount Sinai receiving the laws, the people began to get very impatient. He was such a very long time; would they ever see him again? They felt that if they lost Moses, they would also lose his God as he was the mouthpiece, the link between God and them, a God they could not see. In their desperation they asked Aaron to make them a God they could see, one like the other nations had.

Aaron took their gold earrings, and made an idol cast in the shape of a calf. The Lord saw them worshipping around the idol and sent Moses back to them saying, "

'Then the LORD *said to Moses, "Go down, because your people, whom you brought up out of Egypt, have become corrupt. They have been quick to turn away from what I commanded them and have made themselves an idol cast in the shape of a calf. They have bowed down to it and sacrificed to it and have said, 'These are your gods, Israel, who brought you up out of Egypt.'*

"I have seen these people," the LORD *said to Moses, "and they are a stiff-necked people. Now leave me alone so that my anger may burn against them and that I may destroy them. Then I will make you into a great nation."*

'But Moses sought the favour of the LORD *his God. "*LORD,*" he said, "why should your anger burn against your people, whom you brought out of Egypt with great power and a mighty hand? Why should the Egyptians say, 'It was with evil intent that he brought them out, to kill them in the mountains and to wipe them off the face of the earth'?*

Exodus

"Turn from your fierce anger; relent and do not bring disaster on your people." (Exodus 32:7-12)

However, Moses was ready to plead with God not to let His anger burn against His people. Moses argued that if all the people died there in the desert, the Egyptians would say that He had taken them out of Egypt with evil intentions. Also, that He had a covenant with Abraham, Isaac and Israel (Jacob) that He would make their descendants as numerous as the stars in the sky and would give the land of Canaan to their descendants as their inheritance forever. The Lord accepted his plea and relented and did not bring about the threatened disaster.

When Moses was far enough down the mountain to see that their idolatry had led to revelry and immorality, he too was very angry and flung the stone tablets inscribed with the law, from him so that they broke into pieces – symbolizing the people's lawlessness. He melted down the idol and poured the molten metal into their water, powdered the gold. and made them drink it. What had been given to them by pagans would be turned back to them.

Aaron had lost complete control of the people and so it was necessary to restore order, before they became the laughing stock of neighbouring nations. He told them that God would have them decide that day who was for the Lord and to step forward. Only the Levites (the priesly clan) did as Moses commanded and were therefore told to take a sword and go throughout the campsite wielding it and killing all whom they came across. This resulted in the death of about three thousand because of the sin in their midst. The next day Moses told the people that they had committed a great sin, but, he was going to return to the Lord to try and make atonement for their sin.

Exodus

When Moses met with the Lord he confessed their sin and sought forgiveness for them or for the Lord to accept his life on behalf of them. This proposal was not accepted, the people would be punished as a consequence of their own sin with a plague.

Moses had to plead with God again, this time that God's presence in the camp, leading them on would not be substituted with an angel and on this occasion too Moses won the day and established that God's presence would be with them throughout the journey. In fact, Moses set up a special tent just outside the camp where he would meet with God and on such occasions the Lord hovered over "the tent of meeting" in a pillar of cloud and when all the people saw this pillar of cloud they stood at the entrance of their tents and worshipped the Lord. "The Lord would speak to Moses face to face, as a man speaks with his friend."

'The LORD would speak to Moses face to face, as one speaks to a friend.' (Exodus (33:11)

Such was the loving concern of God for His creation, but, there had to be a willingness to obey and a realization that true love goes hand in hand with justice; unless evil was eradicated, it would overrun all of society. It was important that the people should see and learn God's laws for successful living, so Moses returned up the mountain for another set of stone tablets.

God wanted the people to have a special place in which to worship Him – a Tabernacle. Moses received from Him very detailed instructions as to how the people were to prepare the materials and to construct it. It was indeed an amazing construction to go up in the desert, but it must be remembered that the Egyptians were so glad to see them going that to placate their God they showered them with the very best of their belongings. All this material and jewellery was now being put to good use. Moses asked the whole Israelite community to bring a free will offering to the Lord for the Tabernacle.

'Those presenting an offering of silver or bronze brought it as an offering to the LORD, and everyone who had acacia wood for any part of the work brought it ……….. All the Israelite men and women who were willing brought to the LORD freewill offerings for all the work the LORD through Moses had commanded them to do.' (Exodus 35:24 and 29)

The response of the people was so overwhelming that the skilled workers had to ask Moses to stop the people bringing anymore because what they had was more than sufficient to finish the job.

Not only were detailed instructions given to construct a place for worship, but also for the form of worship. The tribe to which Moses and his brother Aaron belonged, the Levites, were singled out for the honour of being in charge of everything to do with worship, Aaron, himself, was the High priest and his sons were to assist him in his priestly functions.

Other families in the tribe were designated as musicians, singers, servers within the tabernacle, those who packed the tabernacle and its contents up and those who carried it. There was work to do for the whole tribe and only that tribe was involved. When on duty within the tabernacle they wore special garments which were kept specifically for that purpose.

Everything, whether people, instruments, utensils or clothing, was set apart, that is made holy, for the Lord in a special service of dedication. The people had to learn how to respect and reverence the Lord as one set apart from all other gods; and yet had a deeper relationship with them than any other god worshipped by the surrounding nations had with their worshippers, no other god had a visible sign of his presence amongst his people as did the God of the Israelites.

'Then the cloud covered the tent of meeting, and the glory of the LORD filled the tabernacle. Moses could not enter the tent of meeting because the cloud had settled on it, and the glory of the LORD filled the tabernacle. In all the travels of the Israelites, whenever the cloud lifted from above the tabernacle, they would set out but if the cloud did not lift, they did not set out – until the day it lifted .So the cloud of the LORD was over the tabernacle by day, and fire was in the cloud by night, in the sight of all the Israelites during all their travels.' (Exodus 40:34-38)

Leviticus

In this chapter I want to examine the remaining three books which Moses wrote. As with Exodus these books have to do with the time the Israelites spent in the wilderness. It was a prolonged period because when they left Sinai, Moses sent twelve men to explore Canaan, the land God had promised them and to bring back a report. On their return they came bearing a pole to which was attached a single branch of grapes so heavy it took two to carry it, plus pomegranates and figs. They said to Moses

"We went into the land to which you sent us, and it does flow with milk and honey! But the people who live there are powerful, and the cities are fortified and very large." (Numbers 13:27b – 28b)

Their verdict was overturned by two members of the team Caleb and Joshua who felt that with God with them they should go up and take possession of the land. The other team members scoffed at the idea saying,

"We can't attack those people; they are stronger than we are." (Numbers 13:31)

And they spread among the Israelites a bad report.'

Such lack of faith in their omnipotent God was evidence that they were not ready to take the final step, so God turned them around and caused them to wander deeper into the Wilderness. During these years all who were above the age of twenty at the time of this rebellion died in the wilderness even as they had spoken out, except for Joshua and Caleb.

Leviticus

This period of being educated into how God wanted them to live, begins in 'Leviticus' with the tribe of the Levites. They were the tribe set apart by God to lead the people in worship, as a means of showing their gratitude for all that God had done for them. He expected something from them as an acknowledgement of all that He had done in liberating them and providing for their every need.

Whereas Exodus speaks of God's approach to man, Leviticus speaks of man's approach to God. It is a fitting follow on from Exodus although for the Gentile, it is not nearly as interesting because it deals solely with God's instructions to this one tribe. Here we have the word of God literally more than in any other book of the Bible. Again and again we read, "The Lord said to Moses "

"You are to be holy to me because I, the LORD, am holy, and I have set you apart from the nations to be my own."(Leviticus 20:26)

The first few chapters of Leviticus have to do with the sacrifices, both animal and grain, which the Israelites were to offer to God. Most of them had to do with the seeking of forgiveness for sin and guilt. They were never allowed to take sin lightly for it was a barrier between them and God. The life of an animal was given that they might be free from their sins; the cost must reflect true repentance. God made it clear that even unintentional sin required sacrifice, not an excuse. God repeated one lesson over and over, sin must be treated seriously. It is an offense against God which must be made right.

Other offerings were the fellowship or peace offering given as a thanksgiving offering which could take the form of

Leviticus

a burnt offering or a grain offering. In the former offering there are parts of the animal for the priests, some of it eaten by the one offering it as a meal before the Lord and anything left must be completely burnt up.

The next section of Leviticus has to do with the priesthood – their consecration which included cleansing with water, special garments, anointing with oil and a further consecration using the blood of a bull, and rams which was sprinkled on utensils and furniture as well as on the priests, who had to remain in the tabernacle for seven days. All these instructions are given in great detail so that both the priests and the people would have no excuse for not knowing what in God's eyes holiness was and how they should attain it.

It could mean the difference between life and death for them. In fact two of Aaron's sons, Nadab and Abihu were guilty of playing with their censers and offering profane fire before the Lord which He had not commanded them. This fire rebounded back on them and burnt them to death.

'Moses then said to Aaron, "This is what the LORD spoke of when he said: "Among those who approach me I will be proved holy; in the sight of all the people I will be honoured." Aaron remained silent.' (Leviticus 10:3)

Unless His people had a deep respect and reverence for their Lord, they would lose their faith in His omnipotence and Omniscience and their God would be to them as the gods around them, without power or knowledge. "Without faith it is impossible to please God, because anyone who comes to Him must believe that He exists and that He rewards those who earnestly seek Him.

The following few chapters deal with the subject of cleanliness. There were certain living creatures which God

Leviticus

considered unclean and must never be part of their diet and even those creatures it was safe for them to eat must be prepared in specific ways.

Not only were they given detailed dietary laws, but also their clothing, housing and health might cause them to be unclean and need special procedures to render them clean again. It was crucial for them to understand the difference between holy and common, clean and unclean; holy and unclean things must never come into contact, for if there is a mixture of the two, both would become unclean. Only by sacrifice can you cleanse what is unclean and bring it to life.

There was one day of the year, known as 'the Day of Atonement' on which there was a corporate cleansing of the whole nation. This required two goats presented to the Lord at the entrance of the tabernacle.

Lots were cast for the two goats – one for the Lord and the other for the scapegoat. The Lord's goat was sacrificed as a sin offering, but the scapegoat was presented alive before the Lord to be used for making atonement by laying the priests hands on its head and confessing over it all the wickedness and rebellion of the people. Then the goat must be sent away into the desert carrying on itself all their sins. The man in charge of releasing the goat must wash his clothes and bathe himself before coming back to the camp.

The latter chapters of Leviticus are concerned with the way the people lived before each other and especially before God.

'The LORD said to Moses, "Speak to the Israelites and say to them: I am the LORD your God. You must not do as they do in Egypt, where you used to live, and you must not do as

Leviticus

they do in the land of Canaan, where I am bringing you. Do not follow their practices .You must obey my laws and be careful to follow my decrees. I am the LORD" (Leviticus 18:3 - 4)

There follows a series of laws relating to sexual relationships and further details regarding the Ten Commandments. The punishments for breaking these laws were death by stoning or burning in most cases. It was the only way a just God could instil into His people a true sense of holiness, for only a holy life could bring true happiness, a satisfying meaningful life.

Always there was an opportunity for forgiveness through repentance and sacrifice. In Leviticus we have more of the direct speech of God than in any other book of the Bible. For that reason alone, it is an important book to read, if we want to understand the ways of a loving and holy God. Because of His truly caring love for them, He gave them a way of life which would keep them from sickness and poverty. He would defend and protect them if they put their faith in Him and His laws.

Numbers

The book of Numbers starts and finishes with a census. The rest of the book deals with the narrative of the thirty eight years of wandering in the wilderness after they left Mount Sinai interspersed with further instructions from God on a number of issues. 'The Lord said to Moses,' is repeated again and again.

When the people found their circumstances hard they were soon complaining to God whose anger was aroused. Grumbling and complaining were not responses that God expected of them, especially when they suggested that it would be better for them to return to Egypt to enjoy a better diet. God sent fire on the outskirts of the camp which was put out when Moses prayed to the Lord and to satisfy their craving for meat, He sent an abundance of quail to last a whole month, but also a plague. The wilderness became a testing ground for them, where they were learning what it meant to be in a covenant relationship with God.

The law told them what they should do, but it did not change their behaviour, even Moses failed. It was a mammoth task leading a querulous people whose bad attitudes made life so difficult for him. Eventually he lost patience with them when they were wailing about the lack of water so that he did not follow God's instructions carefully. God told Moses to speak to the rock to cause the water to flow out, but Moses, angry with the people struck the rock hard twice so that the water gushed out.

'But the LORD said to Moses and Aaron, "Because you did not trust in me enough to honour me as holy in the sight of the Israelites, you will not bring this community into the land I give them." (Numbers 20:12).

The leaders had to learn to lead as God directed.

Numbers

As they neared the Promised Land, they were attacked by the Canaanites. They called on the Lord, promising that if they could rely on God's help to conquer the people, they would utterly destroy the towns. Their victory was complete. However, as they travelled on their way the people became impatient. Once again they found fault with God and Moses for not providing tasty food and water. God's response was to send venomous snakes in their midst which bit them and many died.

The people acknowledged their sin and asked Moses to pray to the Lord to take the snakes away. The Lord tested their faith in Him by telling Moses to make a bronze snake and put it on a pole. Then when anyone was bitten by a snake and looked at the bronze snake, he lived.

They requested safe passage through the territory of the Amorites, but this was denied them instead their King marched his army out into the desert to attack the Israelites. The Israelites were victorious, capturing their cities to settle there. Their next battle was against King Og of Bashan and his army. The Lord promised them success if they treated them as they did the Amorites which they did.

When the Moabites realized what had happened to their neighbours they summoned help from Balaam of Syria, asking him to come and curse the Israelites. His curses had been very powerful in the past in the bringing down of nations. However, curses do not work on nations blessed of God. Balaam had to help the Moabites some other way.

He suggested they brought pretty girls in to the Israelite camp to seduce them. Most of the illicit sex took place outside of the camp. But one man Zimri brought a girl right up to the Tabernacle. Only one man, Phinehas was so zealous for the Lord's reputation, that he took a spear and pinned the couple to the ground. He was determined to defend God's house against what was happening in God's sight. God rewarded him with perpetual priesthood for him and his family.

The punishment for their sin might seem harsh but God was preparing the nation to enter the Promised Land. When there, the Israelites would find themselves in the midst of most immoral peoples who had fertility goddesses, occult statues and all kinds of licentious behaviour. They needed to know that such things were abominations before God There is much to learn about God's character from the book of Numbers, especially of His loving kindness in supplying all their needs and in enabling them to have victory over those nations who were intent upon wiping them out. We are also shown a very stern God when through lack of faith in Him, they failed to please Him.

Moses has given us a very full account of the ways of his people as well as the ways of His God. In the New Testament, Paul writes to the Corinthians, that they should take heed of what was written in Numbers about the many failures of their ancestors in the Wilderness.

"Now these things occurred as examples to keep us from setting our hearts on evil things as they did. ....
These things happened to them as examples and were written down as warnings for us, on whom the culmination of the ages has come. So, if you think you are standing firm, be careful that you don't fall! No temptation has overtaken you except what is common to mankind. And God is faithful; he will not let you be tempted beyond what you can bear. But when you are tempted, he will also provide a way out so that you can endure it." (1 Corinthians 10:6, 11-13).

Deuteronomy

The book of Deuteronomy was written by Moses during his last days on earth. He was handing over his leadership to Joshua, his second in command. Those whom Joshua was to lead over the river Jordan into the Promised Land had been mere children when the Ten Commandments had been given at Mount Sinai. Except for Caleb and Joshua all their parents had died in the wilderness so that now that Moses was taking his leave of them it was time to remind them of what God expected of them as they set up home in the land they were to possess.

The title of the book, two Greek words, deutero second and nomos – law explains what Moses intended to do, namely give a second reading of the ten commandments plus a number of the 613 laws already given. The children of Israel never had an excuse for not knowing what their God required of them.

"These commandments that I give you today are to be on your hearts. Impress them on your children. Talk about them when you sit at home and when you walk along the road, when you lie down and when you get up. Tie them as symbols on your hands and bind them on your foreheads. Write them on the door-frames of your houses and on your gates." (Deuteronomy 6:6-9)

When they were safely over the Jordan, then Moses commanded, they should erect large stones cover them with plaster and write on them all the words of this to law. They were to be set up on Mount Ebal, as also an altar of stones and offer burnt offerings to God. Fellowship offerings were also to be sacrificed and eaten with rejoicing in the presence of the Lord. The tribes were to be divided into two lots; half to stand on Mount Gerizim to bless the people and half on Mount

Deuteronomy

Ebal to pronounce curses. The blessings would come as a result of their obedience to the commands given them. They would be blessed in the city and countryside and at home.

> *"The LORD will grant that the enemies who rise up against you will be defeated before you. They will come at you from one direction but flee from you in seven." (Deuteronomy 28:7).*

However, with disobedience come the curses.

> *"The Lord will send on you curses, confusion and rebuke in everything you put your hand to, until you are destroyed and come to sudden ruin because of the evil you have done in forsaking Him. ....*
> Then the Lord will scatter you among all nations, from one end of the earth to the other...
> *Among these nations you will find no repose; no resting place for the sole of your foot. There the Lord will give you an anxious mind, eyes weary with longing, and a despairing heart. You will live in constant suspense, filled with dread both night and day, never sure of your life." (Deuteronomy 28:20; 65 - 66).*

Many of the laws given were to combat the fertility practices of the pagan nations surrounding them. Always God's intention in giving them was to promote a happy and healthy life style. They show that God is interested in the whole of our lives; He wants us right in every area of our lives.

At the end of the book we have a beautiful song that Moses gave to his people. A song that records their history, but, also warns of what the future could hold for them if they turned their backs on their God and followed the pagan ways of their neighbours.

> *"In a desert he found him,*

in a barren and howling waste.
He shielded him and cared for him;
he guarded him as the apple of his eye,
like an eagle that stirs up its nest
and hovers over its young,
that spreads its wings to catch them
and carries them on its pinions.
The LORD alone led him;
no foreign god was with Him.
He abandoned the God who made him and rejected
the Rock his Saviour
the LORD saw this and rejected them
because He was angered by His sons
and daughters
"I will hide my face from them," He said
"and see what their end will be;
for they are a perverse generation,
children who are unfaithful".
(Deuteronomy 32: 10-12; 15; 19-20)

The feelings of God toward those whom He chose to be His people, are so powerfully expressed here that who could doubt the love their God had for them and for all who chose to be His child?

"and rejected the Rock his Saviour
the LORD saw this and rejected them
because He was angered by His sons
and daughters
"I will hide my face from them," He said
"and see what their end will be;
for they are a perverse generation,
children who are unfaithful".
(Deuteronomy 32: 10-12; 15; 19-20)

Joshua

In the opening chapter of 'Joshua' we have God's commission to him as leader of His nation to take them into the land of Canaan, possessing it and distributing the inheritance amongst the tribes. It was an awesome task, but, God made as great a promise to him as He had to Moses.

"No one will be able to stand against you all the days of your life. As I was with Moses, so I will be with you; I will never leave you nor forsake you. Be strong and courageous, because you will lead these people to inherit the land I swore to their ancestors to give them." (Joshua 1:5-6).

Several times when speaking with Joshua, God encourages him to be strong and of good courage. Fear would be his biggest enemy as it hinders faith. He, too, like Moses had to learn to trust God implicitly and step out in faith, despite the circumstances.

"Have I not commanded you? Be strong and courageous. Do not be afraid; do not be discouraged, for the Lord your God will be with you wherever you go."(Joshua 1:9)

Always the choice to fear and fail or to hear God properly was his!

It was a new generation that Joshua was called to lead. In the wilderness they had not received the covenant sign of circumcision as had their parents, so that before stepping forward into the land it was necessary for them to undergo this rite. This reminded them of the covenant and to whom they owed allegiance, namely the Lord their God. God also encouraged them by performing the miracle of allowing them to cross over the river Jordan on a dry river bed

They had, therefore, every reason to believe that the God of Joshua was the same all powerful God of Moses and they were willing to give Joshua their undivided loyalty. Joshua, too, had to be prepared for his place in the rank of command. Before the first battle against Jericho he was challenged by the 'Commander of the army of the Lord'.

'Then Joshua fell face down to the ground in reverence, and asked him, "What message does my Lord have for his servant? "(Joshua 5:14).

Joshua knew that he was secure under God's leadership and was ready to hear His plan of attack. When Joshua told his people of God's plan which was very unusual in that it involved marching around the walls of the city rather than any direct attack, they were ready to follow his instructions without question. The walls fell and they were able to walk right in and destroy all that was therein,

'They devoted the city to the Lord and destroyed with the sword every living thing in it– men and women, young and old, cattle, sheep and donkeys.' (Joshua 6:21)

God enabled them to conquer Jericho, but as the first fruits of war against evil, God was to have all the silver, gold and vessels of bronze and iron. The people were told this and all, but one, were obedient to this command. In subsequent victories the loot was divided out between them. However, the next battle against Ai was lost.

Joshua was distraught and sought God for an explanation. He was told there was sin in the camp, which had not been repented. By means of casting lots, the guilty family were found and were stoned to death. His family were

Joshua

implicated in that they knew what he had done and had not reported it. The people were being taught that total obedience alone brings victory. A second attack on Ai, once the sin had been dealt with, brought victory.

In all the battles to take the land, it was a matter of cooperation between God and the people; God would not go ahead without them, and they knew no success without Him.

On one occasion they were hoodwinked into believing the tribe of Gibeonites and were deceived into making a peace agreement with them because they did not seek God's advice on the matter. However, when the Gibeonites were attacked by five kings and their armies God told Joshua to go ahead and support them by attacking their adversaries. They did gain victory by their sword, but as many of the enemy were fleeing, God rained down hailstones on them so large that more were killed by the hailstones than had been in battle.

As battles cannot be fought once the sun has set, Joshua showed great faith by requesting God, before all his army, to stop the sun in the sky and thus give him an extra day to complete his victory. God certainly answers such faith!

At the end of his life, Joshua summoned all his leaders to prepare them for the time ahead. At that time they were enjoying a period of rest whilst settling into their tribal territories which had been allocated to them.

Joshua reminded them that they still had alien nations around them whose way of living and false gods were not to be embraced by them. They were a holy nation, set apart to worship and serve the one true God and so it was forbidden to intermarry with other nations who would draw them away from their God. Moses had given them the law which they must adhere to for in being obedient to that, they would keep faith with their God

Their response was very positive and all witnessed each other to be in agreement. Joshua then warned them,

"He will not forgive your rebellion and your sins, if you forsake the Lord and serve foreign gods. He will turn and bring disaster on you and make an end of you, after He has been good to you." (Joshua 24:19b-20).

Judges

The book of Judges is God's story of how He disciplined His wayward people. Whilst the leaders who had known Joshua were still alive, there were battles fought and won and land secured with God's help. However, once that generation had passed on, the Israelites seemed happy to settle down with the Canaanites. The Angel of the Lord spoke to them of their disobedience.

'When the angel of the Lord had spoken these things to all the Israelites, the people wept aloud.' (Judges 2:4).

The Lord left the nations in the land so that He might test His people as to their obedience to the commandments He had given them. They proved to be a very fickle people who took the daughters of these gentiles to be their wives and gave their daughters to their sons and served their gods, completely forgetting the Lord their God. This aroused the anger of the Lord so that He sold them into the hands of their enemies.

When the Israelites cried out to God, He had mercy on them and raised up a deliverer from their midst. With the help of the Holy Spirit, he was able to lead them to victory in battle and establish peace until his death. For the next two hundred years or so this was the cycle of events – the people did their own thing oblivious of God's laws, suffered defeat at the hands of the enemy because of it and then in their distress called upon the Lord their God to rescue them.

The judges had very different personalities and even morals.

From Gideon the warrior with great spiritual insight and faith. The intrigue and political manoeuvrings of Abimelech a spiritually corrupt judge.

Through to the famous Samson with his spiritual strength but spiritual and moral laxity.

This is a book of human nature at its best and worst through how they lived, plotted, loved betrayed and so much more.

God always answered their cries for help with a new deliverer full of the Holy Spirit who would hear from God the tactics to bring about victory.

Here we see how a caring and loving God disciplines His people, but their distress touches His heart so that their prayers are always heard. In His mercy He answers them.

Ruth

The book of Ruth belongs to the same time period as the book of Judges. It tells of a family, who during a period of famine where they lived in Bethlehem, decided to emigrate to the neighbouring country of Moab. Here the two sons find themselves Moabite wives. Then after a while the father and both sons die, leaving the mother with her two foreign daughters-in-law. She suggests that as she is too old to have any more sons, they should go back to their families to seek further husbands. One agrees, but the other insists that she wants to stay with her mother-in-law.

'But Ruth replied……"Where you go I will go, and where you stay I will stay. Your people will be my people and your God my God. Where you die I will die, and there I will be buried. May the Lord deal with me, be it ever so severely, if even death separates you and me." (Ruth I: 16-17).

Ruth, a gentile, had a desire to serve the God of the Israelites and to show Him the same loyalty that she was expressing toward her mother-in-law, Naomi. They returned to Bethlehem as the famine was over. Here Naomi told the townsfolk that the Lord had greatly afflicted her and was the cause of her misfortune, even though the family had not consulted Him when choosing to leave the country. Once they went their own way, they were no longer under God's protective hand!

They had returned at the time of barley harvest and Ruth was happy to go gleaning on the fields behind the harvesters. The owner of the fields where she was gleaning was Boaz, a relative of her late father-in-law, with whom she found favour. He made sure she had an ample supply of grain to take home to Naomi who, when hearing whose fields Ruth had been in, explained that he was a close relative, a kinsman redeemer.

Ruth

Naomi was keen to give Ruth a chance to become wife of Boaz.

A woman could not propose marriage, but, she could show that she was interested by warming a man's feet. Naomi suggested that Ruth should go secretly to the threshing floor where Boaz would be winnowing barley. When he laid down there for the night she was to uncover his feet and lie down there. Ruth agreed to obey her mother-in-law.

When he awoke and found her, she requested that he spread his garment over her since he was her kinsman. He was happy to do so, but spoke of a nearer kinsman who should have the first offer of her hand. If he refused he would be honoured to have her as his wife.

In the hearing of ten elders, Boaz speaks to this kinsman that he might like to purchase the family land plus Ruth. He is unwilling to do so, which meant Boaz was free to marry Ruth and redeem her land. They had a son named Obed who became the father of Jesse, the father of King David. Ruth as great grandmother to King David is therefore included in the genealogy of Jesus Christ by Matthew (Matthew I: 5)

This piece of Israelite history was probably written.down by Samuel, the prophet, to prepare the way for David to be king.

Here we see in Ruth the characteristics of loving, concern and loyalty, so closely connected, as one is not possible without the other. Father God, too, is ever loyal to His people because of His love for them.

1 Samuel

In these two books, we have the history of the last judge, also a prophet and of the rise and fall of the first two kings. As we read them, we can see how God works with these leaders of their nation, encouraging their skills and disciplining their failures. Always there are honest, detailed accounts of good and bad characteristics.

Samuel, who was dedicated by his mother to be in full time service to the Lord, was taken to live in the house of God at Shiloh when a very young child. Here he ministered before the Lord under Eli the priest. Whilst he was still quite a young lad, God spoke to him. At first he did not recognise God's voice and thought Eli was calling him, but under instruction from Eli, he prepared himself for God's message which was to be given to Eli as it concerned God's dealings with his family.

Eli had been told that God was very displeased with the behaviour of his sons, so much so that there would be their having no regard for the Lord by misusing the sacrifices brought by the people and treating the Lord's offering with contempt. Eli's rebuke of their wicked deeds fell on deaf ears and there was no sign of repentance.

"Therefore the LORD, *the God of Israel, declares: "I promised that members of your family would minister before me forever." But now the* LORD *declares: "Far be it from me! Those who honour me I will honour, but those who despise me will be disdained The time is coming when I will cut short your strength and the strength of your priestly house, so that no one in it will reach old age, and you will see distress in my dwelling. Although good will be done to Israel, no one in your family line will ever reach old age. Every one of you that I do not cut off*

and sap your strength, and all your descendants will die in the prime of life." (1 Samuel 2:30-33)

When God spoke to Eli through Samuel, it was to confirm this word as Eli had known of his sons' sins, but, had failed in his responsibility to restrain them. It was a hard punishment indeed, but without such discipline the people would never learn what 'the fear of the Lord', truly meant. The descendants of Eli did continue to be priests, but none lived to an old age. Samuel remained at Shiloh, faithful in his service to the Lord and knew His presence with him.

"All Israel from Dan to Beersheba recognised that Samuel was attested as a prophet of the Lord." (1 Samuel 3:20).

In a subsequent battle against the Philistines things were going badly, so that the elders of Israel were perplexed as to cause. They decided to take the Ark of the Covenant, which contained the stone tablets of the law, and was kept in the house of God at Shiloh, into battle with them as a kind of lucky omen.

When it arrived all the people cheered, for they felt God was with them and certainly their enemies feared the worse. However, when battle commenced, the Philistines had the victory; the Ark of the Covenant was captured, and Eli's two sons were killed. Eli himself, when he heard the news, fell to his death from the stone wall on which he was sitting. God has to be approached and asked for battle instructions, not for the Ark of the Covenant to be used as a talisman.

The ark of God was taken to the Philistine city of Ashdod where it was placed on a shelf next to their god Dagon. A sanctified object cannot be beside that which is unclean and so Dagon fell from the shelf; this happened twice and on each occasion pieces were broken off the idol.

The people of Ashdod, too, had to suffer so that they might learn that the presence of a holy God could not be treated without respect.

Wherever the ark of God went there was an outbreak of tumours. After seven months there was an outcry for the ark to be returned to Israel and they requested their priests to tell them how to do it. They were advised to make five gold tumours and five gold rats, to be given as a guilt offering which would honour Israel's God. These were to be put in a chest which with the ark of God was to be put on a new cart drawn by two cows which had recently calved. The calves were to be penned up whilst the cows had to take the cart into Israel. This they did, not stopping until they reached Israelite territory.

The children of Israel who had the cart come into their midst, greatly rejoiced to see the Ark of the Covenant. They chopped up the cart and used the wood to offer up the cows as a burnt offering, a sacrifice unto the Lord. When the five rulers of the Philistines who had followed the progress of the cart saw this, they knew that it was the ark of God which had caused all their troubles. Some men of the town decided to look into the ark of God and they were put to death.

This shocked the people and they cried out,

"Who can stand in the presence of the Lord, this holy God? To whom will the ark go up from here? "(1 Samuel 6:20).

The ark was moved to another town where it rested in the house of Abinadab, who consecrated Eleazar his son to guard it. There it remained and was a great blessing to the family until well into the reign of David, twenty years later Samuel was close to God and knew that his people would never know victory over their enemies whilst they had false gods in their midst. The people cried unto God to come to their aid and Samuel told them,

"If you are returning to the Lord with all your hearts, then rid yourselves of the foreign gods and the Ashtoreths and commit yourselves to the Lord and serve Him only, and He will deliver you out of the hand of the Philistines. "(1 Samuel 7:3)

So the Israelites put away their Baals and Ashtoreths and served the Lord only.

Samuel then promised to intercede before the Lord for them. Then they fasted and confessed their sins to God. Whilst Samuel was making a sacrifice to God on their behalf and crying to God for His help, the Philistines attacked. God retaliated with loud thunder which threw the Philistines into such panic that they were routed before the Israelites. After the battle was won Samuel set a memorial stone between Mizpah and Shen.

'He named it Ebenezer, saying, "Thus far the LORD has helped us". (Samuel 7:1)

There was no more war between the Philistines and the Israelites during Samuel's life time. He was a judge to all the people until his old age when he appointed his sons in his stead. However, they, like the sons of Eli, were dishonest and accepted bribes and so perverted justice. The elders were not happy with this state of affairs and begged Samuel to give them a king to lead them. Samuel was most upset and prayed to God about it.

'And the Lord told him: "Listen to all that the people are saying to you; it is not you they have rejected, but they

have rejected me as their king. As they have done from the day I brought them up out of Egypt until this day, forsaking me and serving other gods." (1 Samuel (8:7-8)

God told him to prepare the people for what a king would expect of them, in raising an army of servants and of soldiers. He would expect land and tax you and your belongings. It would be no good crying out to God to relieve you of him when his burdens become too unbearable, for God will not answer you.

This advice went unheeded for still they called for a king, so God told Samuel to give them a king and guided him to anoint Saul as the first king of Israel. The people were pleased with God's choice for Saul was an impressive young man, head and shoulders taller than any other person.

At first Saul did well, filled with God's spirit, he led the Israelite army to victory against the Ammonites who had threatened to invade a border town. However, when tested as to his obedience to Samuel, he failed by taking upon himself Samuel's duties of offering up the burnt offering prior to going into battle.

When Samuel arrived and asked what he was up to, he sought to justify his actions. He did not consider he could be wrong, but blamed his men for scattering and Samuel for being late.

"You have done a foolish thing," Samuel said. "You have not kept the command the LORD your God gave you; if you had, he would have established your kingdom over Israel for all time. But now your kingdom will not endure; the LORD has sought out a man after his own heart and appointed him ruler of his people, because you have not kept the LORD's command." (1 Samuel 13:13-14)

His relationship with Samuel from then on, deteriorated. On another occasion, Saul and his army were sent to do battle with the Amalekites who had sought to hinder the Israelites from coming into the Promised Land when coming up from Egypt. Because of the evil of this nation Saul was told to totally destroy the people and everything that belonged to them. Saul decided to keep the best of the sheep and cattle, plus Agag the King.

When Samuel met up with Saul, Saul assured him that his instructions had been carried out. Samuel pointed out that he could hear the sounds of sheep and cattle. Saul refused to own up to his wrong doing, but rather blamed his soldiers. These animals were kept back to sacrifice them to the Lord. Samuel told him that God knew all that he had done. Again Saul spoke of his obedience to God in this matter; he had just saved a few animals and the king.

> "But Samuel replied: (prophetically)
> "Does the Lord   delight in burnt offerings and sacrifices as much as in obeying the Lord?
> To obey is better than sacrifice,
> and to heed is better than the fat of rams.
> For rebellion is like the sin of divination,
> and arrogance like the evil of idolatry.
> Because you have rejected the word of the Lord,
> he has rejected you as king."(1 Samuel 15:22-23)

It was only then, when confronted with these words of how God sees our sin that Saul confessed that he had sinned, but again tried to justify it by saying that he was afraid of the people and so gave into them. Saul begged Samuel to forgive him, but his answer was,

1 Samuel

"He who is the Glory of Israel does not lie or change His mind; for He is not a man, that He should change His mind." (1 Samuel 15:29).

Saul never again had Samuel beside him to tell him God's will concerning his battles. This led Saul, some years after Samuel's death, to seek out a medium, even though witchcraft had been strictly forbidden by God. He requested that the medium would call up Samuel's spirit for a final conversation. He was told that the next battle with the Philistines would be his last.

The last task that God gave Samuel was to appoint the second King of Israel. He was sent to visit Jesse, a man with eight sons. Seven of them were lined up before Samuel for his inspection, but none of them met with God's approval. Finally, Jesse was asked to bring his youngest son, David in from the field, God told Samuel to anoint him, secretly. He was to be the king in waiting. Many years were to pass before he sat on the throne, during which time; David underwent many tests to prove his fitness for the task ahead of him.

David's three eldest brothers were in Saul's army and on one occasion David was taking provisions to them when the Philistines put out a challenge to Saul and his army to choose a man who would face up to their champion Goliath and kill him. Goliath was a giant of a man, over nine feet tall. Saul and his army were absolutely terrified. David, however, had spent much time as a shepherd and during the long lonely hours in the field he communed with the Lord God and became familiar with His law.

He learnt to trust His God to give him victory over the wild animals which attacked his sheep. His only weapon was a sling and pebble, but, with much practice he became very skillful in the use of it. David was completely submitted to his God, having great faith that with God on his side, he could do all things. Therefore, when he heard Goliath's challenge, his anger was stirred; how dare an uncircumcised Philistine defy the armies of the living God. He felt that God who had kept him safe and delivered him from wild animals would give him the victory. He told the king as much. As no one else was willing, David went out to face the giant, having refused Saul's armour.

God did not let him down; a single stone knocked Goliath down and David used the giant's own sword to cut his head off. It was such faith that caused God to see in David "a man after mine own heart."

'the LORD has sought out a man after his own heart and appointed him ruler of his people,' (1 Samuel 13:14)

Another pastime of David's was making music on his harp, and this skill brought him into Saul's court as the king's personal musician. Saul had lost the Spirit of the Lord because of his disobedience and so was from time to time plagued by an evil spirit. When he was tormented David's calming music soothed him. Saul became very attached to David and requested his father to let him live in his palace. Here he met up with Jonathan, Saul's son and the two became the best of friends.

As David matured Saul was very pleased with him and gave him a high rank in the army where he was very popular. However, David's popularity with the people who sang his praises, really angered Saul. He became very jealous of the young man so much so that he twice threw a spear at him, but David eluded him. Saul was afraid of David because he realized God was with him, and not the King. It was David who led the troops into battle.

1 Samuel

His successful campaigns caused the people to love him even more. Saul was hoping the Philistines would wipe him out in battle, but when this seemed unlikely he asked his son Jonathan and all the attendants to kill him. Jonathan was far too fond of David to obey his father, but he did warn David.

It was soon necessary for David to go in hiding, so he sought out Samuel and stayed with him. Jonathan was ready to relay his father's movements to David and keep him one step ahead.

On two occasions, David with his followers had the chance to kill Saul when he was in hot pursuit to kill David. However, when David crept up to him unnoticed and was about to lay his sword on him, he became conscience stricken saying,

"The Lord forbid that I should do such a thing to my master, the Lord's anointed, or lay my hand on him; for he is the anointed of the Lord." (1 Samuel 24:6)

Nor would David allow his men to attack Saul.

On the second occasion, too, David had ample opportunity to take Saul's life or allow his men to do so, but he could not bring himself to do so. He does let Saul know of the opportunity he had, and asks him, why he is so keen to take his life. Saul confesses his sin. David replied,

"The Lord gave you into my hands today, but I would not lay a hand on the Lord's anointed. As surely as I valued your life today, so may the Lord value my life and deliver me from all trouble."(I Samuel 26:23-24)

David was on the run from Saul for many years during which time he was able to train up a very effective,

1 Samuel

well disciplined army from the malcontents who joined him in hiding. He even had the audacity to take refuge with the Philistines, the arch enemy of Israel. All the while, his relationship with his Father God was growing. Never once did he blame God for his uncomfortable circumstances; always when he was up against it he sought wisdom from God as to what best to do.

The final battle against the Philistines into which Saul led his army, was a case in point. Those who sheltered David and his men expected them to fight on the Philistine side. At the last moment, however, David and his men were sent back to the Philistine town where they had left all their wives, children and belongings.

On arrival there, they found to their utter dismay that the Amalekites had taken advantage of the absence of the Philistines and had raided their towns. All that David's party had left behind was gone. The men were so grief stricken at their loss that they were ready to take their anger out on David, by stoning him.

'But David found strength in the Lord his God.'
(1Samuel 30:6)

He enquired of God what to do next; should he pursue the raiding party? God gave him assurance that he and his men should do so and would have success. It was not an easy task and some of his men were too exhausted to continue the whole way. David agreed to leave them and went on with the rest.

They came across an Egyptian slave of the Amalekites whom they revived and he gave them directions to reach the raiding party who were off guard, reveling in all the plunder they had taken David fought them all the next day, succeeding in recovering everything that had been taken from him and his men plus much else. When they returned to the exhausted men, those who had fought the battle with him, wanted to give them only their lost belongings. David, however, full of God's Spirit, had a much more generous attitude.

His reply was,

"No, my brothers, you must not do that with what the LORD has given us. He has protected us and delivered into our hands the raiding party that came against us. Who will listen to what you say? The share of the man who stayed with the supplies is to be the same as that of him who went down to the battle. All shall share alike."

David made this a statute and ordinance for Israel from that day to this. (1 Samuel 30:23-25).

2 Samuel

The news that Saul and Jonathan had died in battle was not received by David with great joy as his friends expected. He mourned their death and wrote a lament to be sung by the people. He knew that with God on his side, he could be very generous towards his onetime enemy as well as his best friend. David lamented.

> *"Saul and Jonathan – In life they were loved and gracious, and in death they were not parted.*
> *They were swifter than eagles, they were stronger than lions.*
> *How the mighty have fallen! The weapons of war have perished!"* (2 Samuel 1:23; 25; 27).

When David enquired of God where he and his men should settle, he was told to go to Hebron. Here they settled with their families, and it was here that the men of Judah approached him to become their king. He was King of Judah in Hebron whilst Saul's son Ish-Bosheth was King over the other tribes for two years.

The war between the house of David and the house of Saul lasted a long time. During this time David grew stronger.

When Abner, the commander of Ish-Bosheth, was killed after he had agreed with David to change sides, David was truly upset and would not condone his death. In fact he put on sack cloth and took part in the funeral, weeping at his tomb. Ish-Bosheth, too, was murdered and his head brought to David, but as with Saul, David did not rejoice, but was angry that an innocent man should be killed whilst asleep in his own house. He ordered his men to put the murderers to death and had Ish-Bosheth buried. David's magnanimity of spirit, so pleased the people that the elders of Israel anointed David king over Israel seven and a half years after he had become king in Hebron. One of his first tasks was to capture Jerusalem from the Jebusites and make it his capital city. God was with him in battle because he was always eager to know God's will in the matter. However, as to his private life, his marriages, he indulged his weakness on this matter with no recourse to God and took to himself many wives and had many children. These were to give him great trouble in his life.

David also saw God's hand against him when he tried to bring the Ark of the Covenant into Jerusalem. He made plans to have it brought into the city on a new cart escorted by himself and thirty thousand chosen men. These plans were made without any referral to the instructions for its carriage given by Moses. When they set out from the house on a hill where it had rested for the last few years, David was in high spirits and he and all with him celebrated with much music and dancing.

At one point the oxen stumbled, so one of the men put out his hand to steady the ark; an irreverent act which God punished by striking the man dead David and all his men could not understand why God would do such a thing and began to fear Him. He decided not to take the ark any further and left it in a nearby house. Here it remained for three months and was a great blessing to the family. The next attempt at bringing the ark to Jerusalem was made according to the instructions of Moses. The ark was carried by the Levites on poles especially made for the purpose. David was learning the hard way to respect the word of God in the handling of holy objects.

There was still much rejoicing that the ark was being restored to the special tent of worship that David had for it in Jerusalem; music and dancing accompanied its journey and David participated in the dancing with all his might even though his wife, Michal, considered his actions far too vulgar for a king.

David wanted to honour the Lord by building a temple in which to keep the Ark of the Covenant as well as for a place for the nation to worship. However, word came to him from the Lord to say that the temple would be built by his son when he was on the throne. God promised him that his house and kingdom would endure forever. From his many victories over the nations surrounding him, David gathered much precious materials, all of which he dedicated to the Lord, to be stored up for use in the building of the Temple.

There were occasions when David neglected his military duties leaving his commander-in-chief to lead his men to victory. During this period he lusted after another man's wife and so that he might have her, David arranged for the husband to be killed. God spoke to David through the prophet, Nathan, saying that his evil acts would be punished for God is very aware of all that we do.

In breaking God's law, David was despising his Lord. As a result he would never have rest from battle; calamity would come upon him out of his own household. What is more David would receive his punishment in full view of the nation, though he had sought to keep his sin secret.

David repented and acknowledged that his sin had been against his God. Nathan replied,

"The LORD has taken away your sin. You are not going to die. But because by doing this you have shown utter contempt for the LORD, the son born to you will die." (2 Samuel 12:13-14)

2 Samuel

The sin of his children caused David great grief, especially that of Absalom, a favourite son. He sought to gain the favour of the people in order to usurp the throne from his father. David had to flee Jerusalem with his entire household.

When David sent out his troops to do battle with those of Absalom, he made them promise to bring Absalom back alive. He loved his son too much to contemplate his death. However, in the course of action Absalom was captured and against the advice of David, was put to death. It was news David did not appreciate hearing and his mourning for his son was loud and long.

This upset his army chief who felt that his king had not shown his army the gratitude due to them for saving his life and throne. It was necessary for David to make peace with his men and to return to Jerusalem to be accepted again by his people. Even as God had forgiven him, so he, in turn, forgave the people of their disloyalty.

David knew, too, his relationship with his Lord God, had enabled him to pull through this family disaster. His gratitude to his God is beautifully expressed in the song of praise he wrote at this time. He said:

> *"In my distress I called to the LORD;*
> *I called out to my God,*
> *From His temple He heard my voice;*
> *my cry came to His ears.*
>
> *at the rebuke of the LORD,*
> *at the blast of breath from His nostrils,*
> *He reached down from on high and took hold of me;*
> *He drew me out of deep waters.*
> *He rescued me from my powerful enemy,*

From my foes, who were too strong for me.
They confronted me in the day of my disaster,
But the LORD was my support,
He brought me out into a spacious place;He rescued me because He delighted in me."
(2 Samuel 22:7; 16b-20)

    Why did God delight in David? Was it not because of David's faith in Him? This steadfast faith like that of his forefather Abraham was counted to him for righteousness.

1-2 Kings

Even on his death bed, David had trouble with his family in securing the son of God's choice on the throne, but he did live to see his son Solomon anointed King in his place. His final words to Solomon were that he should observe what the Lord his God requires; that he should walk in His ways and keep His decrees, laws and requirements as given by Moses in order that he might experience a prosperous reign. He also spoke of God's promise to him that He would always keep a descendant of David's on the throne of Israel, if and the condition was important, the descendants

"If your descendants watch how they live, and if they walk faithfully before me with all their heart and soul, you will never fail to have a successor on the throne of Israel." (1 Kings 2:4)

At the beginning of his reign, Solomon was eager to do just that, 'to walk in God's ways.' When God visited him one night in a dream and offered to give him anything he asked for, Solomon's request was for wisdom. He acknowledged before God how young and ignorant he was, so he requested,

"Give your servant a discerning heart to govern your people and to distinguish between right and wrong. For who is able to govern this great people of yours?" The LORD was pleased that Solomon had asked for this." (1 Kings 3:9.10).

Not only did God give him wisdom, but also riches and honour, so that he would be greater than any other king. If he continued to walk in obedience to God, he would also have a long life. Solomon certainly saw this promise come true. It was said of him that his wisdom was greater than that of all the men of the East and that included Egypt. His fame soon spread to all the surrounding nations and his knowledge of the natural world was very profound. Men from all over the world were coming to hear his wise sayings Solomon means 'peace' and indeed there was peace during his reign.

As God had promised David, Solomon was able to build a temple for his God with all the materials that his father had faithfully collected for it. It took seven years to build, the first permanent building for centralized worship. When it was completed and all Israel gathered to worship within, Solomon gave the prayer of dedication. This prayer started with a declaration of God's greatness, kindness and reliability to the promises He has made. Solomon reminds Him of what He has said concerning himself and his descendants and the conditions of the promises.

He then asks for the people of Israel especially concerning the forgiveness of their sins when they come before God with repentant hearts. He quotes many of the laws of Moses as found in Leviticus and Deuteronomy reminding the people of their covenant with God and their responsibilities in the keeping of it. There is also a plea for the foreigner or gentile who might visit the land and want to worship the Israelite God that they might receive answers to prayer made in the Temple. He ends by declaring before God and the people that it was God who set them apart from the rest of the world to be His own heritage and therefore should be ever attentive to their cries to Him.

God appeared a second time to Solomon as before and spoke of His acceptance of this dedicatory prayer with the promise that;

"I have consecrated this temple, which you have built, by putting my Name there forever. My eyes and my heart will always be there." (1 Kings 9:3).

God also promised that Solomon's descendants would always be on the throne, as long as His conditions were kept. However, if these conditions were ignored, then 'though this temple is now imposing, all who pass by will be appalled and will scoff and say,

"Why has the LORD done such a thing to this land and to this temple?" People will answer, "Because they have forsaken the Lord their God, who brought their ancestors out of Egypt, and have embraced other gods, worshipping and serving them – that is why the Lord brought all this disaster on them." (1 Kings 9:8b-9)

Solomon had shown great wisdom when dealing with the problems of others. His recorded advice was of great benefit to many, but he showed very little wisdom in his own private affairs. As with his father, he had a great weakness where women were concerned; the number of his wives and concubines was legendary.

Many of his alliances were of a political nature to establish a peace treaty with his neighbours. These foreign wives, however, brought with them their own gods and culture. They needed their own places of worship to be built, outside the city walls certainly, but these gradually led the people astray and indeed Solomon himself who was toward the end of his reign making more and more compromises. God could not look on his sinful life and without Him, his joy departed, leaving a frequently depressed and cynical being.

At his death, his son, Rehoboam succeeded him. Rehoboam has been influenced by his father in his latter years; a father with a divided heart, left a son with shaky foundations. Rehoboam did not think to go to God for wisdom on how to rule his people. He sought it firstly from his father's elders, and as their advice was not pleasing to his ears, he then went to his godless companions. Their advice to act as a tyrant and demonstrate his power was far more acceptable. This policy however, brought rebellion and the ten northern most tribes soon found a leader to enable them to break away and have their own kingdom.

Their leader, Jeroboam, had been a leader under Solomon, when he received a prophecy that the Lord was going to punish the sins of Solomon by taking away most of the kingdom, ten tribes, from his son. These ten tribes would be given to Jeroboam who would have a secure inheritance for his descendants if he lived and ruled according to God's law and with His help. Solomon heard of this prophecy and tried to kill Jeroboam, but he escaped to Egypt, only to return when he heard of Solomon's death.

From this time onward, at least five hundred years, there were two kingdoms; the Kingdom of Judah, with the tribes of Judah and Benjamin, in the south and the Kingdom of Israel with the other ten tribes in the north. The southern kingdom had Jerusalem and the temple within its borders which was a great attraction to those in the north who were loyal to their God. Jeroboam realized this and set up an alternative place of worship in two places, one in Bethel and the other in Dan in which he placed a golden calf and announced to the people that these would be their gods.

'And this thing became a sin; the people came to worship the one at Bethel and went as far as Dan to worship the other.' (1 Kings 12:30)

His priests were appointed from amongst all the tribes, even though they were not Levites. He even instituted a festival to coincide with the festival held in Judah

There were sacrifices offered on an altar built at Bethel, sacrificing to the calves. God did send a man from Judah to warn Jeroboam of his evil and that the wrath of God would one day be brought down upon this altar at Bethel. Jeroboam put out his hand to seize the man but, God caused his hand to shrivel up so that he could not pull it back. The altar was split in two and the ashes spilled out. The King begged the prophet to intercede with God that his hand might be restored, which he did and the hand was restored.

Despite this graphic warning, Jeroboam did not change his ways and he continued to use priests at the altar who were not Levites. His complete disregard for God's holiness led to his personal downfall, and that of his descendants too.

When his son became ill, he sent his wife in disguise to the prophet at Shiloh, to find out what would happen to the boy. God prepared the prophet for her coming so that he was able to greet her by name. The prophet told her that God had seen all the wickedness of her husband whom God had honoured by giving him the kingship over the northern tribes, but he had chosen to disabuse this sacred trust in him,

"You have made for yourself other gods, idols made of metal; you have provoked me to anger and thrust me behind your back. Because of this I am going to bring disaster on the house of Jeroboam." (1 Kings 13:9-10).

She was told that the child would die and all Israel would mourn him and he would be buried; the only one of his family to be buried. God would raise up another king. She was also warned that all the people of Israel would suffer because Jeroboam had led them into the sin of idol worship. Allegiance to God and His laws was no better in the southern Kingdom of

Judah. Here, too, the people and their king did what was evil in God's eyes so provoking Him to anger.

'There were even male shrine-prostitutes in the land; the people engaged in all the detestable practices of the nations the Lord had driven out before the Israelites.' (1 Kings 14:24.)

As a result God allowed the King of Egypt to attack Jerusalem. He carried off all the treasures of the temple and the King's palace. However, because of His promise to David, 'a man after His own heart who confessed and had his sins forgiven, God gave the throne to the son of Rehoboam. His reign was very short as he indulged in all the sins of his father.

' his heart was not fully devoted to the LORD his God, as the heart of David his forefather had been.' (1 Kings 15:3b)

In the northern nation of Israel the kings were all bad, but some were worse than others. These were twenty kings in all, before God finally put into action the curse that Moses had warned about, and many subsequent prophets had reiterated, namely that if the people abandoned their God, turning their backs on His laws, they would be sent into exile.

The Kingdom of Judah also had twenty kings. However, not all of these kings were bad for at least six were good and two very good. They had just one dynasty whereas Israel had nine. On the whole the good kings reigned longer, seeking God's help to do so. This resulted in Judah remaining a kingdom, one hundred and forty years longer than their northern counterpart. Eventually their cup of evil was full, and they too were exiled. The books of Kings not only records details of the kings of the two kingdoms, but also includes the history of two prophets, Elijah and Elisha, in greater detail than most of the kings. They were both concerned with revealing to the northern Kingdom the God whom they should be worshipping; His power and supremacy over all other gods.

Elijah was first sent to Ahab, a very evil King who was under the sway of his wicked wife, Jezebel. Elijah came with a warning that there would be no rain for the next few years until Elijah spoke it into being.

During this time God directed Elijah to a place where he would be fed by ravens and drink from a brook. God supplies all the needs of His children if they are obedient to His directions. When the brook dried up, Elijah was told to go to Sidon, beyond the borders of Israel where a widow was willing to share with him what she thought was her last piece of bread. Because of her faith in Elijah and the words of his God, her supply of flour and oil did not run out until rain was restored to the land. Sometime later the woman's son died and she thought Elijah was the cause.

"What do you have against me, man of God? Did you come to remind me of my sin and kill my son?" (1 Kings 17:18).

Elijah answered her queries by taking the dead child to his room and pleading with God to return life to the boy. He then lay on top of him, three times. The Lord heard his cries and the boy's life was restored, as also was the faith of the woman;

"Now I know that you are a man of God and that the word of the Lord from your mouth is the truth." (1 Kings 17:24)

God's miracles always encourage faith, but also reveal His loving kindness toward us. Perhaps the greatest miracle which God performed through Elijah took place on Mount Carmel. Elijah had confronted the King, Ahab, when the latter had accused him of being a trouble maker in the land.

"I have not made trouble for Israel," Elijah replied. "But you and your father's family have. You have abandoned the LORD'S commands and have followed the Baals." (1 Kings 18:18)

Elijah finished this very bold statement by issuing a challenge to the four hundred and fifty prophets of Baal who were kept by the queen. They were to meet Elijah on Mount Carmel and also all the people of Israel. Elijah declared to his fellow countrymen that this was an opportunity for them to make up their minds as to whom they would serve;

"How long will you waver between two opinions? If the LORD is God, follow him; but if Baal is God, follow him." (1 Kings 18:20)

Elijah knew that it is impossible to serve the Lord God and anything else; there is no compromise with the Lord God. The people did not reply so Elijah gave the details of the challenge; each side was to build an altar for the sacrifice of a bull. The prophets of Baal were to go first by calling upon the name of their god to bring down fire on their altar to burn up the sacrifice. Elijah would follow this by calling on the name of the Lord. The god who answered by fire would be seen as the true God.

The prophets of Baal spent all day calling, but to no avail. Throughout their ordeal, Elijah mocked them, such was his great faith that his God would triumph. He was not deceived in his belief, for despite the fact that his altar was drenched with water, when he called, God answered with fire to burn up the sacrifice, wood, stones and soil.

1-2 Kings

'When all the people saw this, they fell prostrate and cried, "The LORD – He is God! The LORD – he is God!" (1 Kings 18:39)

The prophets of Baal were put to death and Elijah warned the King that rain was coming, so he had better get home. Elijah was left to plead with God to cause the rain to fall. The power of the Lord upon Elijah was such that he was able to run through the rain down the mountain side, overtaking the King in his chariot.

When the queen heard of the fate of her prophets she was determined to have Elijah put to death. Surprisingly the man who had stood alone before four hundred and fifty prophets of Baal, was afraid of this woman, and ran for his life. He escaped through the southern kingdom down into the desert. Here he sat under a tree and pleaded with God to take his life, until he fell asleep.

God sent an angel to feed him, after which he slept again until woken up by the angel with another meal for him. Strengthened by the food he continued on his journey to Mount Horeb. Here he took refuge in a cave. In the morning, he heard God's voice asking him what he was doing in this place. His reply was full of self- pity, seeking to justify his actions;

"I am the only one left, and now they are trying to kill me too." (1 Kings 19:10b).

God told him to go out and stand on the mountain in His presence. Whilst there he experienced a mighty wind, an earthquake, a fire but God was not in any of these. Then he heard a gentle whisper – the voice of God, who again asked him what he was doing there. He replied in the same vein as before. God spoke to him of work to do, so he must return.

However on the way, he would meet up with his successor, Elisha, whom he was to train to take his place. His cry that he was on his own was untrue; there were seven thousand in Israel, who had not bowed the knee to Baal or shown any allegiance to him.

Once Elijah had fulfilled his service to his Lord and Elisha was ready to take on the responsibility assigned him, God took Elijah up into heaven in a chariot of fire, in a whirlwind. He was only the second person to escape death.

Elisha was a prophet in touch with the people, more so than Elijah. Moses had given to the Levites the task of keeping the people in the knowledge of the true worship of their God and of relaying His word, the law to them. However, since the kingdom was divided, in the north there was little evidence of the Levite tribe fulfilling this duty. It was left to the prophets, especially Elijah and Elisha to bring the word of God to them.

It was important, therefore, that they were respected and given the honour due to a spokesperson for God. When Elisha was mocked by a group of youths, such behaviour merited a curse from God; it was a serious offence. With God's protection removed, the youths were open to an attack of bears who mauled them to death. However, those who honoured the prophet and sought his advice, they were rewarded.

On his visits around the country, Elisha met the needs of those whose water supply was bitter, by performing a miracle of healing it with the aid of a bowl of salt.

A widow of one of the prophets received from him, the help needed to keep her sons from becoming slaves. As he journeyed around, a rich woman urged him to stay for a meal. Whenever he passed that way he would call in and have a meal with her and her husband. They decided to build a room for him to stay overnight. Elisha in return wanted to do something for them, He was told by a servant that the man and his wife wanted a son. and so Elisha asked God for a son for her. The following year the baby was born. However, the child caught sun stroke and died.

The mother knew that only Elisha could help and went in search of him; he immediately responded and returned with her and even as Elijah had done, he prayed over the dead child before laying on him and bringing him back to life.

On another occasion when the land was suffering from drought so that there was a food shortage, Elisha was given twenty loaves of bread. Elisha directed the donor to give it to the people. He felt it was impossible to feed a hundred people with so little, but Elisha told him again to do just that;

"For this is what the LORD says: "They will eat and have some left over." (2 Kings 4:43b)

The hundred enjoyed the bread and as the LORD said, there was some left over.

Such incidents and many other miracles that Elisha performed for the benefit of the people, made them aware that there was a loving God who was eager to meet their needs when they put their faith in Him Elisha was also there when his king needed guidance in time of war. Acting on a word of knowledge, Elisha told the King where the Arameans, who were engaging in battle with the Israelites, were likely to approach. There were several such warnings and the frustrated Aramean King demanded to know who was betraying him.

He was told of the Prophet Elisha's God given ability. The King decided to seek out Elisha and put a stop to him and his tactics. His men found out he was in Dothan and so an army was sent thither with horses and chariots to storm the city. When they arose next morning, Elisha's servant looked out and saw the army surrounding them, he was very afraid and cried to Elisha to help.

"Don't be afraid," the prophet answered. "Those who are with us are more than those who are with them." (2 Kings 6:16).

Elisha prayed that his servant's eyes would be opened; a prayer God answered so that the man saw the hills around the city full of horses and chariots of fire. As the enemy approached, Elisha asked God to strike them with blindness. He then informed them that they were coming to the wrong city, but he would lead them to the man they were looking for, and he led them to the King's palace in Samaria. Once there, the Lord opened their eyes. The King was ready to kill them, but Elisha said that would not be right seeing as he had not captured them fairly in battle. Instead he was to set a meal before them which the King did; a veritable feast was set before them and then they were dismissed to return home.

The Arameans stopped raiding Israel's territory from then on. This is a lovely story of how God was working with His people to demonstrate His loving concern for their welfare.

1 Chronicles

These books were written after the people of Judah had returned from exile in Babylon by a priest, probably Ezra as the style of the writing is very similar to that of the book of that name. Although they cover very much the same period as do the books of Kings, their approach to history is quite different.

Whereas in the books of Kings the author is dealing with the people, God's special people and their attitude to Him and His law, with an emphasis on their sin and God's mercy and forgiveness when they cried to Him.

In the books of Chronicles the author emphasizes the sovereign deliverance of God; how He was true to His word and kept the covenant He had made with them. The purpose of these two books was to encourage the small body of people who were seeking to settle in the land after its devastation, and to exhort them to put their trust in a faithful God. They were to learn from the failure of the past, in order that they might not make the same mistakes.

The author of the book of Hebrews in the New Testament also saw the need for the present generation to learn from the accounts in the Old Testament of Israel's disobedience. (Hebrews 4:11)

The first book of Chronicles begins with the genealogies of the Israelite people from Adam through to those returning from exile. They were certainly biased toward the line of David and the Levite tribe from whom the priests came.

and the Levite tribe from whom the priests came. The purpose of these nine chapters of genealogy was not only to reveal God's faithfulness to His promises to Abraham and

1 Chronicles

David, but also to underline the importance for racial and religious purity. The climax of these genealogies comes in Chapter 9 where it is stated;

'All Israel was listed in the genealogies in the book of the kings of Israel and Judah. They were taken captive to Babylon because of their unfaithfulness. "But Judah was carried away captive to Babylon because of their unfaithfulness."
(1 Chronicles 9:1).

In the next twenty chapters we have the history of the southern kingdom, Judah from a brief account of the end of Saul's reign, through David's reign which is given in great detail. His first exploit as King, recorded in Chronicles, was to take the city of Jebus, referred to as the stronghold of Zion, the city of David. Here he took up residence, having built up the city and its surroundings.

'and David became more and more powerful, because the LORD Almighty was with him.' (1 Chronicles 11:9)

David's success was due to the loyal support of his warriors or 'mighty men' and their details are given so that the people of Judah might feel a link to them.

Having established, Jerusalem as his capital city, David wanted the Ark of the Covenant there too, but his first attempt to do so was without reference to God and His instructions and ended in disaster, but sometime later, a chastened and wiser man, he prepared a tent for it and David declared.

'No one but the Levites may carry the ark of God, because the LORD chose them to carry the ark of the LORD and to minister before him for ever.' (1 Chronicles 15:2)

Below are the joyful words of a man who knew His God

intimately like Moses before him.

"Give thanks to the LORD, call on his name;
make known among the nations what he has done.
Sing to him, sing praise to him;
tell of his wonderful acts.
Glory in his holy name;
let the hearts of those who seek the LORD rejoice.
Look to the LORD and his strength;
seek his face always.
Remember the wonders he has done,
his miracles, and the judgments he pronounced,
you his servants the descendants of Israel
his chosen ones the children of Jacob..
He is the Lord our God;
his judgments are in all the earth.
He remembers his covenant for ever,
The promise he made, for a thousand generations." (1 Chronicles 16:7-15)

.He was aware that the Lord God was not confined to Israel, but was judge of all the earth; His praises were to be spread abroad for all mankind to know of His greatness.

The chronicler records that David, when faced with an invading Philistine army enquired of the Lord whether he should attack them or not; would the Lord be with him and grant him victory. The Lord promised to hand them over to him. The defeated Philistines abandoned their gods on the battle site and David ordered for them to be burnt.

Once more the Philistines raided Israel and again David spoke to God about his tactics in battle. He was told to wait until he heard the sound of marching in the tops of the mulberry tree which they were to encircle. Only at that point were they to strike out. This they did and gained another decisive victory.

'So David's fame spread throughout every land, and the LORD made all the nations fear him.' ('1 Chronicles 14:17')

There were a number of other battles in which David had success, but for him, his greatest project was to build a beautiful temple for his Lord God. He shared this passion with the prophet, Nathan. However, God spoke to Nathan that it would not be David who would build the temple but his son. When this was relayed to David, he took the disappointment very well indeed. Instead of being angry with God, he showed great humility before God and thanked Him for His promise that one of his descendants would be on the throne forever.

David's weakness where women were concerned is glossed over in this book, although the taking of a census without the Lord's direction to do so, is mentioned.

'Satan rose up against Israel and incited David to take a census of Israel.' (1 Chronicles 21:1).

This act of defiance on David's part, led to the whole nation being punished by God. David was horrified by the result of his action and immediately sought God to confess his sin and have His forgiveness. Through the prophet Gad, God put three options to David. David's reply was that he would rather suffer from the hands of God whose mercy was great, than from the hands of men. As a result a plague fell on Israel and seventy thousand men of Israel fell dead.

An angel was sent to destroy Jerusalem, but as the angel began to destroy the people God stopped him in his tracks, saying that was enough. David and his elders saw the angel poised between earth and heaven and they prostrated themselves before God. Again he reminded God that it was

1 Chronicles

he who had sinned and not the people, so that it should be him and his family who suffered. Then the angel ordered Gad to tell David to build an altar on the spot where the angel had stopped.

This piece of land belonged to Araunah, the Jebusite. David wanted to purchase the land from Araunah who was willing to give it to him. He was also ready to give David oxen and threshing sledges for the burnt offerings, plus wheat for the grain offering.

'King David replied to Araunah "No, I insist on paying the full price. I will not take for the LORD what is yours, or sacrifice a burnt offering that costs me nothing." (1 Chronicles 21:24)

He made the altar and God sent fire from heaven on it. Then David decreed that place was to be the site for the temple. Although he would not take part in the building of it, David made very careful preparations for it.

'David said, "My son Solomon is young and inexperienced, and the house to be built for the LORD should be of great magnificence and fame and splendour in the sight of all the nations. Therefore I will make preparations for it." So David made extensive preparations before his death.'
(1 Chronicles 22:5).

In this, as in all things, especially concerning that to do with his God, David set a standard of excellence which his son Solomon adhered to. The book ends with the lists of Levites and priests and the work that they would be doing in the temple. Having given so generously himself to the building of the temple, David then made an appeal to his leaders of the tribes to make a contribution. This they did willingly.

'The people rejoiced at the willing response of their

leaders, for they had given freely and wholeheartedly to the L<small>ORD</small>. *David the king also rejoiced greatly '(1 Chronicles 29:9.)*

David had lived his life openly before his subjects; always singing of the many blessings which his Lord had showered upon him in response to his faith and obedience. They saw in him, how to live before a generous, loving God.

2 Chronicles

In the second book also, the chronicler is most selective in his choice of historical events. The book gives a very detailed account of Solomon's reign because he was greatly blessed of God with wisdom, wealth and honour. To Solomon fell the honour of organizing the building of the temple. In his letter to Hiram, King of Tyre, Solomon wrote; "The temple I am going to build will be great, because our God is greater than all other gods.

'But who is able to build a temple for him, since the heavens, even the highest heavens, cannot contain him? Who then am I to build a temple for him, except as a place to burn sacrifices before him?' (2 Chronicles 2:6)

He began his reign well, with a deep understanding and respect for the Lord he was to serve.

The chronicler makes no reference to his numerous wives who came to Jerusalem with their gods and priests and had to be accommodated with places of worship. They caused Solomon to compromise which led to his heart becoming hardened so that God raised up adversaries to oppose him and to one of them, Jeroboam was given the ten northern tribes.

However Solomon died in peace and it was his son, Rehoboam who witnessed the division of the kingdom. A prophet told Rehoboam not to go to war against Jeroboam and Rehoboam was obedient to this message from God, because of this.

All the Levites came to Judah and Jerusalem, leaving behind the lands given them in the territories of the northern tribes as they were no longer to serve as priests in Jeroboam's Kingdom.

"After the Levites left and sided with Rehoboham. *Those from every tribe of Israel who set their hearts on seeking the* LORD, *the God of Israel, followed the Levites to Jerusalem to offer sacrifices to the* LORD, *the God of their ancestors. They strengthened the kingdom of Judah and supported Rehoboam'* (2 Chronicles 11:16.17)

However once he was established in his kingdom, Rehoboam went his own way, forsaking God and His law and his subjects followed his example. When the King of Egypt came up against Jerusalem, capturing the fortified cities of Judah on his way, the prophet came to Rehoboam and the leaders of Judah with the word of God. They had forsaken the Lord and so He had forsaken them. They were repentant and so God promised not to destroy them, but because of their sinful attitude toward Him, they would be in servitude to the King of Egypt (Shishak)

"They will, however, become subject to him, so that they may learn the difference between serving me and serving the kings of other lands." (2 Chronicles 12:8)

The only incident recorded of Rehoboam's son, Abijah's reign, was a battle against Jeroboam. He had come down upon Judah with twice the number of troops that Abijah could muster. Nevertheless, Abijah stood his ground and declared to the invading army that they were coming against the Kingdom of the Lord; not only that, but they had forsaken the true God for idols using false priests for worship. Judah was not guilty of doing this; indeed daily there is worship in the temple.

"God is with us; … People of Israel, do not fight against

the LORD, the God of your ancestors, for you will not succeed."
(2 Chronicles 13:12a-d).

Their faith was rewarded for God routed Jeroboam and all his army and they suffered heavy losses. The men of Judah knew that they were victorious because they relied on the Lord.

Abijah's son Asa is referred to as a good king for he did what was right in the eyes of the Lord his God. He put away the idols in Judah and removed his mother from the palace as she was worshipping an idol. He also had victory in battle despite a very small army; he declared his faith in God.

'Asa said, "LORD, there is no one like you to help the powerless against the mighty. Help us, LORD our God, for we rely on you, and in your name we have come against this vast army. LORD, you are our God; do not let mere mortals prevail against you." (2 Chronicles 14:11b.)

During his reign many people from the northern tribes of Ephraim, Manasseh and Simeon came over to be part of the Kingdom of Judah when they saw that God was with them and causing them to prosper. However, toward the end of his reign when once more the Israelite army descended on him, he panicked and sent all the silver and gold from the temple to the King of Aram, in Damascus, requesting his help to subdue his invaders. He agreed and attacked Israel from the North, so that the Israelite army returned.

Then the prophet of God (called Hanani) told King Asa that he had been very foolish in relying on the King of Aram rather than on the Lord.

"For the eyes of the LORD range throughout the earth to strengthen those whose hearts are fully committed to him. You have done a foolish thing, and from now on you will be at war."

(2 Chronicles 16:9.)

The result of this would be continual war with his neighbours. Asa put the prophet in prison for these words! Asa's son, Jehoshaphat, was another very good king who sent the Levites into every town to teach the law of God.

He was victorious over Ammon and Moab. Before he went into battle, he went to the temple and before all the assembly he prayed to God, reminding Him of how He had led the nation in the past and had brought them through many battles. He then declared his confidence in God, to reveal to him the tactics in battle which would secure victory:

"O our God, will you not judge them? For we have no power to face this vast army that is attacking us. We do not know what to do, but our eyes are upon you." (2 Chronicles 20:12).

God gave him his instructions via a Levite; assuring him that the battle was his if he was obedient to the Lord's command. They were to take up their positions, but with singers to go ahead of the army.

'As they began to sing and praise, the LORD set ambushes against the men of Ammon and Moab and Mount Seir who were invading Judah, and they were defeated.'
(2 Chronicles 20:22.)

After the battle there was so much plunder that it took three days to collect it! They were richly rewarded for their faith in God.

At the end of his reign, Jehoshaphat allied himself with Ahaziah an evil king of Israel to make ships to go to Tarshish without consulting God and the result was disaster; all the ships were wrecked.

He was succeeded by his eldest son Jehoram who began his reign by killing all his brothers and other princes to stifle any opposition. He was greatly influenced by his wicked wife, Athaliah and between them they unravelled much of the good accomplished by his father.

He was struck down by a foul disease and his son Ahaziah who succeeded him also followed in his footsteps, ignoring the ways of God and was murdered. His mother, the wicked queen, Athaliah, wanted to take the throne of Judah for herself, so destroyed all royal heirs, but the daughter of King Jehoram took Joash the baby son of Ahaziah and hid him from his grandmother. King Jehoram's daughter was the wife of the priest Jehoiada and together they brought up Joash in the temple.

When he was seven, they rallied all the Levites to come to the temple, and the people were informed that the son of the King, of the line of David was to be crowned. When Athaliah heard the noise of the people rejoicing at having a king crowned, she tried to prevent it, but was surrounded by the army and put to death.

Jehoiada the priest then made a covenant that he, the people and the king would be the LORD's people.
(2 Chronicles 23:16)

They smashed all the idols and altars of Baal, and killed their priests and Jehoiada set up temple worship once again, allotting the Levites to their duties even as King David had ordered. Whilst Jehoiada was alive, Joash was a good, law-abiding King, but after his death, he was easily persuaded by some of his officials to allow the worship of false gods.

God sent prophets to him to warn that in forsaking God and His ways, he would not prosper for God would forsake him. Joash, the King even ordered that Zechariah, Jehoiada's son, be stoned to death, because he spoke out against the king's behaviour.

When Judah was invaded by the Aramean army they were defeated and Joash was severely wounded. His son, Amaziah began well, but was not whole-hearted in his allegiance to the Lord and often did his own thing which caused his downfall. Uzziah, his son is referred to as a good king because he organised the building of towers in Jerusalem and in the dessert.

While he sought God during the days of Zechariah, the prophet who taught him to fear God, he prospered. He became a very powerful king and his fame spread far and wide. However, his pride in his achievements let to his downfall. He felt he was above the priesthood and could do their duties in the temple. He was confronted by the priests, but still went his own way, with the result that leprosy broke out on his forehead. He had leprosy until he died, never allowed in the temple again.

Jotham grew powerful because he 'because he walked steadfastly before the LORD his God.'(2 Chronicles 27:6)

However, his son Ahaz, was a king who chose to worship the Baals, even sacrificed his sons in the fire in the valley of Ben Hinnom. God was not with him so that he suffered heavy defeats at the hands of the Arameans and the Israelites who took a large number of Judeans as prisoners.

However, when warned by a prophet that God's fierce anger rested upon them for this act, they returned the prisoners to Judah.

'The LORD had humbled Judah because of Ahaz king of Israel, for he had promoted wickedness in Judah and had been most unfaithful to the LORD.' (2 Chronicles 28:19)

When the son of Ahaz, Hezekiah became king he was eager to bring Judah back into a right relationship with God and so called all the Levites and priests together asking them to sanctify themselves and then to clear out all the rubbish in the temple and sanctify it for use as a place of sacrifice and worship.

Once this was completed, Hezekiah gathered the city rulers together and went to the temple to offer bulls, rams and lambs as a sin offering for the sanctuary and the Kingdom of Judah, and all Israel. Whilst the priests were sacrificing, the King commanded the Levites to play their musical instruments and for the singers to sing so that the whole assembly worshipped the Lord.

Once the service of the temple had been re-established, Hezekiah's next intent was to celebrate the Passover, even if a month late owing to the lack of sanctified priests the previous month.

The King wished to include all Israel in this celebration and so sent invitations to those of the northern tribes who had not been carried off into exile by the Assyrians. He felt that if they humbled themselves before God by coming to the Passover celebrations, then they could renew a relationship with their God and He would soften the hearts of their captors who would be compassionate toward them and would allow them to return to their homeland.

For the most part the couriers who took those invitations

to the northern towns were scorned and ridiculed, although there were some from the tribes of Asher, Manasseh and Zebulun who journeyed south to Jerusalem. However a very large crowd gathered for the celebrations which were such a success that they extended them for a further week. In order that the priests and Levites would be able to continue their service in the temple, Hezekiah ordered the people to start bringing their tithes regularly to the temple, having first set the example with his own generous giving.

"In everything that he undertook in the service of God's temple and in obedience to the law and the commands, he sought his God and worked wholeheartedly. And so he prospered." (2 Chronicles 31 v 21).

When the Assyrian army invaded Judah, Hezekiah sought God's aid to repel them. The Lord sent a deadly disease amongst the Assyrian troops so that those who were spared withdrew to their own land in disgrace.

At the end of his life envoys were sent by the rulers of Babylon to him to find out all that God had done for him and in his pride Hezekiah foolishly showed them all the many treasures of his palace and the temple. All the good work that Hezekiah had done in establishing temple worship according to the commandments of Moses was undone by his son, Manasseh, who when king introduced Baal worship once again into the land. All the wicked practices of child sacrifice, sorcery, divination and sorcery of the pagan nations were introduced by the king.

He did much evil in the eyes of the LORD, arousing his anger. (2 Chronicles 33:6.)

The Lord spoke to Manasseh and his people, but they took no notice, so He allowed the Assyrian king to take him prisoner. In his distress Manasseh did humble himself before the Lord, entreating Him to have mercy on him and God heard his plea and caused him to return to Jerusalem.

'And when he prayed to him, the LORD was moved by his entreaty and listened to his plea; so he brought him back to Jerusalem and to his kingdom. Then Manasseh knew that the LORD is God.' (2 Chronicles 33:13)

He sought to restore the temple, and to remove all the altars on high places and told the people to serve the Lord God. Amon, his son, who succeeded him was as evil as his father had been at the start of his reign. However there was no humbling of him, and in desperation his officials plotted against him and had him assassinated in his palace.

His young son Josiah was made king in his place. He was a good king in that he sought to serve the Lord God by restoring the temple and worship within it. Whilst the Levites were doing a thorough work of restoration, they discovered a book of the Law of Moses which had remained hidden for many centuries.

Josiah was greatly distress by how far the people had strayed from God's ways and was very concerned about the curses which would be brought upon them for disobedience The prophet (Huldah) gave him assurance from God that He saw his heart that he was eager to please Him and that he, Josiah, would not experience the curses during his reign.

'Your eyes will not see all the disaster I am going to bring on this place and on those who live here.' (2 Chronicles 34:28b)

Josiah was also keen to celebrate the Passover at the right time and in accordance with the instructions given by Moses, which with the help of the priests and Levites, he was able to achieve. Unfortunately for him, he chose to go to war with Egypt even though they were not seeking a battle with Judah and in the battle he was killed.

The four kings who followed him had very short reigns; none of them looked to God to help them in their difficulties and so in the last chapter of the book we read of the fall of Jerusalem when the King of Babylon invaded the land and carried off all the articles from the temple and the treasures from the temple and the Kings palace.

The soldiers set fire to the temple and broke down the wall of Jerusalem, destroying anything of value within the city. The remnant who escaped the sword were taken into exile. The land enjoyed seventy years of Sabbath rest until the first year of Cyrus, King of Persia who had defeated the Babylonians and taken over their empire.

Ezra

In the books of Ezra and Nehemiah we read of how the kings of Persia gave permission for the return of the exiled Jews from Babylon to Jerusalem. They came in three returns; the first was when Cyrus was the King of Persia. This had been prophesied many hundreds of years before as had the duration of the Jewish exile before the first return.

On this occasion Zerubabel was the leader of 50,000 Jews; he was of the royal line stretching back to King David and so fulfilling the promise of God that there would always be a descendant of David on the throne, although a governor rather than king. He is also listed as one of the ancestors in Jesus' family tree in Matthew 1.

Just over ninety years later, Ezra led 1,800 exiles back to Jerusalem. He was a priest who brought the scriptures, Genesis to Deuteronomy, with him, and made certain that his party contained Levites who would help him establish the structure of worship once again for the people of Israel.

Fourteen years after Ezra's return, Nehemiah returned with a few craftsmen. He was most concerned with the building of the wall of Jerusalem without which the city was vulnerable to attack. God fulfilled His word spoken previously to Jeremiah by moving King Cyrus of Persia to say;-

"The LORD, the God of heaven, has given me all the kingdoms of the earth and he has appointed me to build a temple for him at Jerusalem in Judah." (Ezra 1:2)

They were to go with gifts from their neighbours of gold, silver, goods and livestock. King Cyrus himself gave to themall the articles of the temple which Nebuchadnezzar had carried away from Jerusalem. Once they had settled in their homes, they all met in Jerusalem to build an altar on which to sacrifice burnt offerings, despite their fear of the people around them. These people were from various conquered nations, who had been drafted in, mainly to the northern Kingdom and had intermarried with the few Israelites who had escaped exile. They were later known as 'Samaritans'.

Two years later, having amassed the materials needed, they began to lay the foundation of the temple. When these were completed, there was great thanksgiving, although emotions were mixed; the older ones who dimly remembered the glory of the former temple, wept aloud whilst many others shouted for joy.

"No-one could distinguish the sound of the shouts of joy from the sound of weeping, because the people made so much noise. And the sound was heard far away." (Ezra 3:13).

The foreigners in the land wanted to help build the temple, but the Jews rejected their offer, so they then did their best to discourage the builders. When this did not work, they sent a letter to the King in Persia, telling of the Jewish activity and suggesting that there was some underhand motive in what they were doing.

Sometime later two prophets came and prophesied to the people of Jerusalem that the work of rebuilding the house of God should go ahead for God was with them. This time when a letter of complaint was sent, a new King of Persia, Darius, searched the archives and found the relevant records of King Cyrus

Darius wrote that the temple must go ahead as a place to present sacrifices. The cost would be met from the royal treasury. The Samaritans were told not to interfere with the building but on the contrary were to aid the building by supplying the revenues collected in their districts. All the sacrificial animals wheat, salt, wine and olive oil were to be supplied daily as well from the same revenues:

"so that they may offer sacrifices pleasing to the God of heaven and pray for the well-being of the king and his sons." (Ezra 6:10).

God's people, when they looked to Him for help, received it in abundance.

The temple was completed six years later and dedicated to God with great joy. There was much sacrifice; the priests were installed in their divisions, and the Levites in their groups for the service of God.

It was after this that Ezra and his party returned, with the permission of the King of Persia, who instructed him to take the silver and gold that the King and his officials had freely given to the God of Israel together with all the silver and gold they might obtain from the province of Babylon. The King wanted the money to be spent on sacrifices both animal and grain offerings.

"You and your brother Jews may then do whatever seems best with the rest of the silver and gold, in accordance with the will of your God....... And anything else needed for the temple of your God that you may have occasion to supply, you may provide from the royal treasury." (Ezra 7:18, 29).

Here again we see God's abundant provision for His people when their hearts are set upon doing His service

Ezra and his party were very vulnerable to attack in their long and difficult journey from Babylon to Jerusalem laden as they were with so much silver and gold. However, Ezra knew he could not ask for protection from the King as he had declared that his God had His hand on all who look to Him, but His great anger is against all who forsake Him. Ezra did not only know his scriptures, but also had the faith to put them into practice.

"There, by the Ahava Canal, I proclaimed a fast, so that we might humble ourselves before our God and ask Him for a safe journey for us and our children, with all our possessions. …. So we fasted and petitioned our God about this, and He answered our prayer." (Ezra 8:21, 23).

One of the first problems that Ezra had to deal with after he arrived in Jerusalem was that of intermarriage. Even the priests and Levites had not kept themselves separate from the neighbouring peoples with their detestable practices.

Ezra was appalled by the state of affairs to such an extent that his reaction was to humble himself before God as a penitent sinner; taking on the sins of his fellow countrymen.

He acknowledged that they had fully deserved the punishment of exile because of the great sins of their forefathers and that by rescuing a remnant of the nation and bringing them back to Jerusalem, God had treated them better than they deserved and now here they were living no better than their ancestors, completely disregarding God's laws.

As he wept and confessed before the house of God a great crowd of Israelites gathered around him and they too began to weep bitterly.

As a result several of the leaders publicly declared their sin and agreed to put away their foreign wives and children. Ezra put these leaders under oath to do what they suggested and while he fasted before God, he asked all the exiles to gather

Ezra

in Jerusalem or forfeit their property. When all were gathered in the square, Ezra addressed them, speaking of the sin of intermarriage and their need to confess it. Then he declared they were to separate their foreign wives. All agreed to do this

Nehemiah

The book of Nehemiah begins with his prayer to God on behalf of his fellow countrymen who had made the journey back to Jerusalem. He, like Ezra, was devastated to hear the news which had filtered back to him from Jerusalem, how that they city wall was broken down and its gates had been burnt. Nehemiah was an important person in Susa, capital of Persia, as cupbearer to the King. His immediate reaction was to speak to God about it;

"O Lord, God of heaven, the great and awesome God, who keeps His covenant of love with those who love Him and obey His commands, let your ear be attentive and your eyes open to hear the prayer your servant is praying before you day and night for your servants, the people of Israel. I confess the sins we Israelites, including myself and my father's house, have committed against you. We have acted very wickedly towards you. We have not obeyed the commands, decrees and laws you gave your servant Moses." (Nehemiah 1:5-7).

He went on to request the favour of the King whom he was serving. This was indeed granted him for the King was only too happy to give him leave of absence to go to Jerusalem with letters to give him both safe conduct there, plus the provision of the materials required for the building of the wall.

On arrival in Jerusalem, Nehemiah made a close inspection of the wall and its gates by night. Having decided what needed to be done, he rallied the priests and officials and told them of his plans inviting them and all the people to join him in the rebuilding of the walls. They were eager to get started. Their enemies, when they heard of the matter, mocked them, accusing them of rebellion against the King. Nehemiah's answer was a confident one of faith. He said.

Nehemiah

"The God of heaven will give us success. We, His servants, will start rebuilding, but as for you, you have no share in Jerusalem or any claim or historic right to it." (Nehemiah 2:20).

God had chosen in Nehemiah a man fully equipped for the job. He wisely chose families to build up a portion of the wall near to where they lived. He was not only the administrator but also a fellow worker and in no time at all the wall had reached half its height. This so incensed their enemy that they threatened attack. Nehemiah's response was to pray to God,

"Hear us, O our God, for we are despised. Turn their insults back on their own heads. Give them over as plunder in a land of captivity. Do not cover up their guilt or blot out their sins from your sight, for they have thrown insults in the face of the builders." (Nehemiah 4:4).

Having prayed to His God, Nehemiah posted a guard day and night to meet the threat. Gradually the builders began to feel the task was too great for them, and so Nehemiah rallied his people to encourage them, reminding them that the great and awesome God was on their side and the work they were doing was to protect their homes and families.

He then arranged for half of his men to do the work whilst the other half were equipped with spears, shields, bows and armour. Officers were posted behind all the people who were building. Those who carried materials did their work with one hand, and held a weapon in the other. The trumpeter was stationed with Nehemiah and when his trumpet was sounded all would come to that spot. The wall was completed in fifty two days!

"When all our enemies heard about this, all the

surrounding nations were afraid and lost their self-confidence, because they realized that this work had been done with the help of our God." (Nehemiah 6:16).

Besides the rebuilding of the wall, Nehemiah also sought to rebuild the morale of the people. The rich were getting richer and the poor, poorer due to the financial transactions which contravened the Mosaic Law. People were being crippled with debt through the high interests the money lenders were charging on their loans.

Nehemiah bravely addressed these issues and sought to bring an end to such practices. The other great problem was that no one wanted to live inside the city, for they feared attack. They found it easier to hide in the countryside. Nehemiah had to compel people to live in the city, mainly by persuading families whose forebears had lived there, to settle where their roots were.

Whilst Nehemiah was in Jerusalem, as governor of the land, Ezra read the Book of the Law of Moses, to the people and also explained it to them. As they heard it they wept, but Nehemiah encouraged them to stop weeping as the day was a festival, a time of rejoicing unto the Lord.

'Nehemiah said, "Go and enjoy choice food and sweet drinks and send some to those who have nothing prepared. This day is sacred to our Lord. Do not grieve, for the joy of the Lord is your strength." (Nehemiah 8:10).

Later that same month, they gathered to confess their sins, having first heard the Book of the Law being read. Although all who confessed also signed an agreement to keep the law and not to allow their sons and daughters to intermarry amongst the surrounding nations, this agreement was soon broken when Nehemiah returned to Susa.

Nehemiah

On his return to Jerusalem he found a Samaritan family actually living in the temple accommodation. He quickly threw out the man and his belongings and had the room purified. He also found that the Levites had not been given the portions assigned to them and so had had to work in the fields to earn a living. Because of this:

'.he rebuked the officials and enquired, "Why is the house of God neglected?" Then I called them together and stationed them at their posts.' (Nehemiah 13:11)

There was also a widespread neglect of the Sabbath rules which he had to put right, reminding the nobles of Judah that they were stirring up the wrath of God against Israel if they flouted His rules.

Esther

The book of Esther is the romantic story of a beautiful Jewish lady who through great courage is able to keep the Israelite race alive.

Although this book does not mention openly the name of God, yet we can see His hand in all the events as they occur. However for the Hebrew readers who love acrostics they would be aware of the name of the Lord, HVHJ on four separate occasions in the book, and EHYH = 'I am' on another.

The story is wholly set in the Persian city of Susa many years after the Jews made the first exile from Babylon to Jerusalem. At that time the royal monarch was King Xerxes, who ruled over an empire stretching from India to Egypt. Many Jews still lived throughout this vast empire, having chosen not to return to Jerusalem.

The King had gathered all his military leaders to a conference in Susa to discuss a possible invasion of his territory by Greece. When this week long conference was over, the King threw a banquet for his leaders in the garden of his palace and for entertainment summoned his queen to dance; she flatly refused to do so. In order not to lose face he dismissed her as queen. Later a search was made throughout the land for the most beautiful girl to replace the banished queen.

Esther lived with her cousin, Mordecai who had adopted her as his daughter, because she was an orphan. She was chosen to go to the palace and undergo the year-long beauty treatments before being presented to the King. Mordecai had cautioned her not to mention that she was Jewish as there was at court an arch enemy of the Jews, Haman, a noble close to the King, who could make trouble for her if he suspected her nationality.

Esther was the firm favourite of the King and was duly crowned queen. Mordecai kept in daily touch with her and so was frequently at court. Haman was so proud of his position before the King that he insisted that everyone should kneel down and pay him honour; Mordecai refused. At last Haman had an excuse to go to the King and suggest that the Jews living in his empire should be annihilated.

He explained to the King that these people the Jews were different from all other people and did not obey the King's laws, so it was not in the King's best interest to tolerate them. He proposed having them destroyed, and bribed the King to his way of thinking, by offering ten thousand talents of silver to pay all the men sent to do the job. The King agreed that he should do with the Jews as he pleased.

In the first month of the year a lot (Hebrew 'pur') was cast as to when the Jews were to be annihilated and it fell on the twelfth month, the thirteenth day. Dispatches were went by couriers to all the provinces, notifying the people of this order and that they should be ready on the set day to carry it out and plunder the goods of all the Jews.

If Haman's wicked plan had taken place and all the Jews wiped out then God would not have had a people prepared for His Son. This was not in His will, so circumstances were put in place to prevent it happening.

When Mordecai learnt of the plan, he tore his clothes and put on sackcloth and ashes. In this garb he was unable to enter the palace grounds for it was forbidden.

Esther was told by her maids of Mordecai's distress and

Esther

she sent him clothes which he refused, but he told the maids of the situation and sent a copy of the text of the edict and told her to go to the King to beg mercy and plead with him for her people. She sent her official back to him to say that if she went into the King's presence without being summoned she would be put to death, unless the King extended his golden sceptre to her

'Mordecai's reply was, "Do not think that because you are in the King's house you alone of all the Jews will escape. For if you remain silent at this time, relief and deliverance for the Jews will arise from another place, but you and your father's family will perish. And who knows but that you have come to royal position for such a time as this?"(Esther 4:12-14).

'Then Esther sent this reply to Mordecai: "Go, gather together all the Jews who are in Susa, and fast for me. Do not eat or drink for three days, night or day. I and my attendants will fast as you do. When this is done, I will go to the king, even though it is against the law. And if I perish, I perish." (Esther 4:15 -16).

Esther approached the King, the golden sceptre was extended to her and the King was willing to hear her request to have him and Haman to a banquet that she had prepared for them. On the first occasion when they attended her banquet she requested that they came again on the morrow.

In the meantime Haman returned to his family and friends boasting of his elevation by the King above all other nobles and of how the Queen had honoured him but the one fly in the ointment was the Jew Mordecai who still sat at the King's gate. They suggested to him that he had a gallows built and then they should ask the King's permission to hang Mordecai on it. This pleased him very much.

Esther

That night the King found it hard to sleep, so he ordered for the book of the Chronicles, the record of his reign, to be brought to him to read. In this book was recorded an incident of some time ago when Mordecai had discovered a plot to assassinate the King and he had exposed it. The King was reading about this on this particular night. He enquired what honour or recognition Mordecai had received for this.

The reply was nothing.

When Haman arrived to speak about Mordecai and the gallows the King asked him how he should honour a man who had pleased him. Haman, sure that the King was referring to himself, replied that he should be dressed in royal robes, put on a royal horse and led around the town by a noble prince.

To his horror the King told him to do all he suggested for Mordecai and lead him through the town, proclaiming how pleased the King was with him.

That afternoon Esther again entertained the King and Haman. On this occasion too, the King enquired what favour he could grant his queen. The Queen replied that she would ask for her life, and that of her people.

"For I and my people have been sold to be destroyed, killed and annihilated. If we had merely been sold as male and female slaves, I would have kept quiet, because no such distress would justify disturbing the king." (Esther 7:4).

The King was so angry when he heard that it was Haman who had plotted to do this, that he left the room and went to his garden. Haman stayed behind to beg the Queen for his life and was falling on the couch on which the Queen was reclining when the King entered. The King accused him of molesting her. One of the King's eunuchs told him of the

Esther

gallows built for Mordecai who had helped the King. The King ordered Haman to be hung on it; his estate was given to Esther and the King's signet ring, previously worn by Haman was given to Mordecai.

Esther again pleaded with the King, falling at his feet and weeping. She begged him to put an end to Haman's evil plan. The King replied that a document sealed with the King's seal cannot be revoked, but if they were to write another document which would give the Jews in every province the right to assemble and protect themselves, then they could destroy any armed force which might come against them. This was sent out in the third month. The Jews struck down all their enemies with the sword.

In these three books, Ezra, Nehemiah and Esther we read how the Jewish nation and its religion were kept alive by a remnant of people who steadfastly kept their faith in their God and His power to support and maintain His people against all odds.

Those who returned from exile to Jerusalem found it very hard not to blend in with the surrounding peoples, accepting their culture and thus ceasing to be a people set apart for the glory of God.

However, men like Ezra and Nehemiah and other faith filled prophets encouraged and set the example for their brethren to follow. Satan almost had victory when Esther was on the throne in Persia. Here again, God had His faithful followers who were willing to fast and pray to allow His plans to be put into operation. It was the courage and obedience of one woman who saved the whole nation from being wiped out

Job

The book of Job is part of the 'Wisdom' literature in the Bible, along with Psalms, Proverbs, Ecclesiastes and The Song of Solomon. The author of Job is unknown but probably lived at the time of Moses somewhere in the Mesopotamian Basin, around the Rivers Tigris and Euphrates beyond Damascus. This is where he set his story, based on the true suffering of a God believer, but written as poetry and so the facts have been embroidered somewhat.

It is a philosophical book, answering all the main questions of life, but especially, why do good people suffer? How can a loving heavenly Father allow His children to endure the agonies of mind and body inflicted upon Job?

It is therefore a theological book in that it relates all questions to God for the author believes there is one God who relates to His creation; that He is almighty, all-powerful and all-knowing; and that He is good, caring and compassionate. Why, if these characteristics are true, does He allow the innocent to suffer? This is an important book in opening up the theme of my book.

The first and second chapters are a prologue, giving the setting of the story. Satan meets with God and challenges the piety of Job, as follows

'the LORD *said to Satan, "Have you considered my servant Job? There is no one on earth like him; he is blameless and upright, a man who fears God and shuns evil.' "Does Job fear God for nothing?" Satan replied. (Job 1:8-9*

Satan infers that God has so rewarded Job with family and wealth and has put a hedge around him that his faithfulness is to earn this. But if everything he has is

Job

removed, he would curse God. God knows that Job loves Him for Himself alone, and so agrees to Satan removing family and belongings.

Job mourns his loss, but still worships God, acknowledging that all he has was given by God and therefore He has a right to take it away but He still deserves to be praised.

When Satan meets up with God again, God points out that Job still maintains his integrity despite his loss. Satan replies that he still has his good health but if that was taken from him, surely then he would curse God.

God agrees to Satan attacking Job's physical body, though not to take his life. Satan afflicts Job all over his body with painful boils. Job retires to the ash tip and his wife tells him to curse God and die! Job's reaction to all this?

"Shall we accept good from God and not trouble?" (Job 2:10).

At this point in the story no one on earth knew what God had sanctioned in Heaven. Job was visited by three friends, probably older than him who out of respect for his grief sit with him in silence for a whole week. Job was the first to speak and he did so by cursing the day he was born; had he died at birth, he would now be at peace in sheol. His question to his friends was,

"Why is light given to those in misery, and life to the bitter of soul?" (Job 3:20).

Job

His three friends each spoke three times with Job, on the question as to why Job was suffering more than other people.

First came the elder statesman, Eliphaz who quite gently spoke with Job of his belief that one received punishment for sin based on the doctrine of reward and punishment. Job must have sinned, otherwise why the punishment. Job's punishment was merited by his behaviour; no one can say he is innocent before God, since all have sinned. Job must agree that his sin is the reason for his pain and that suffering was God's way of making him a better person. Job would not accept this, so Eliphaz became more impassioned in his argument, claiming that Job was obstinate to insist on his innocence and indeed he was irreverent.

Eliphaz resented Job's opposition to his views and eventually his sympathy wore out and he pointed out that since all mankind were depraved he had no right to grumble about suffering. The wicked did not prosper and even if they did they were not happy. He spoke of God as being beyond our understanding and reach; not concerned with the lives of individuals like Job. He should not expect God's attention.

The second of the three to speak, Bildad, was the theologian, full of clichés and jargon. He had little patience or compassion for Job. He told him that he lost his children because they were sinners who deserved God's wrath.

Bildad believed in a moral universe with the law of cause and effect applying to moral as well as material life. He too said that if you sin, you suffer so Job must be a pretty bad sinner. He told Job that he was talking nonsense and asked Job if he had forgotten that God was all-powerful and that we cannot argue with Him, so why not just accept his fate.

Zophar, the third friend to speak was the most dogmatic of the three. He accused Job of talking to cover up his guilt. If he was not consciously sinning, then he must be sinning unconsciously. He insulted Job by telling him to make a choice between good and evil and that he would be rewarded when he started along the right road. All three friends had basically the same argument; suffering was the punishment for sin.

Job replied to all the speeches of each one of them and to the young man, Elihu, who was the last to express his opinion.

Job never doubted in all his answers to his friends that God was responsible for his suffering and that he could not be made to repent because he was not aware of any sin he had committed. He had sort to live his life in obedience to God's will. During his answers he did swing between despair and hopelessness on the one hand and confidence and hope on the other.

He asked God to leave him alone and yet he talked frankly and honestly with Him too. He would like to take God to court as he claimed that he could win a case against Him. He boldly proclaimed his faith in an afterlife where he would meet God who would redeem him.

He spoke of his intimate friendship with God who filled him with wisdom so that he could give counsel to those who needed it. God too supplied his wealth that enabled him to meet the needs of the poor.

Nothing or no one came before God in his affection and the keeping of God's laws was his greatest delight. In no way was there reason for his suffering as far as his behaviour was concerned.

When Elihu finally got a chance to speak he claimed to bring the latest ideas to the debate on suffering but despite his many words they did not add up to much more than had already been expressed; that Job must have sinned. God has spoken to men in various ways such as dreams, visions, etc., and suffering was God's method to speak to Job to save him from himself. His solutions to the problem were no more adequate than that of the previous three speakers.

During his speeches, Job had asked God many times to speak to him and at last he got his wish. God spoke to him out of a storm, reminding Job that He is the creator and sustainer of the whole universe.

"Where were you when I laid the earth's foundation? Tell me, if you understand." (Job 38:4)

He then asked Job if he could match this work, or if he had the right to judge Him. Should God explain Himself to him? Job was made to feel very small and he confessed that he had no right whatsoever to question God.

"Will the one who contends with the Almighty correct him? Let him who accuses God answer him!" Then Job answered the LORD: "I am unworthy – how can I reply to you?" (Job 40:2-5)

God appeared to him on a second occasion out of a storm and asked Job about his thoughts on the behemoth or hippopotamus and the leviathan or crocodile. The one who made them understands them and can control them. Is Job up to this? Job was being reminded that he could not understand the animal world, so how could he understand the

God who made them! Therefore he had no right to try and argue with God.

'Job replied, "I know that you can do all things; no plan of yours can be thwarted. You asked, 'Who is this that obscures my counsel without knowledge?' Surely I spoke of things I did not understand, things too wonderful for me to know." (Job 42:2-3).

Job's reaction was to despise himself and repent in dust and ashes.

God then spoke to Eliphaz, letting him know that he was angry with him and his two friends as they had not spoken the truth concerning Job. He told them to go to Job and sacrifice a burnt offering for themselves and Job would pray for them that God would not deal with them according to their folly.

After Job had prayed for his friends, God made him prosperous again. His wealth was twice that of former times and God also granted him many children again and a very long life, full of happiness.

God never did answer the question about suffering fully neither to Job or his friends. Nor did He explain His pact with Satan. What they did come to understand was that suffering was not always caused by sin although it could be. However there is a purpose in all the suffering that God allows, even if we do not understand it here on this earth. If sin and suffering were directly related we would be forced to be godly for purely selfish reasons. God wants us to have the opportunity to love Him for Himself; because we desire a relationship with Him and through Him a relationship with our neighbour.

Psalms

The Book of Psalms is the hymnbook and prayer book of Israel in the Old Testament. It is the longest book in the Bible and took about a thousand years to write, although most of the psalms were written at the time of David

They cover the whole gamut of human emotions; the negative feelings of anger, frustration, jealousy, despair, fear and envy and also the positive feelings of joy, excitement, hope and peace. The psalmist expresses exactly how he thinks and feels. They were intended for anyone and everyone to use in their worship of God.

The themes include the history of Israel, from creation to the return of the exiles to Jerusalem. Many are inspired by a personal experience. In fact the main circumstances of David's life are depicted here; for instance Psalm 3 was written by David when he was fleeing from his son Absalom. David is refreshingly honest. He curses men, complains about God and asks for revenge on his enemies. However each negative comment is made to God. He tells God exactly how he feels and what he thinks.

Many of the psalms are to help people in their personal walk with God. For instance Psalm 119 was written to encourage us to read the Bible, and Psalm 92 to encourage us to keep the Sabbath or a day, set apart for God. Other psalms are best taken together as a group, such as Psalms 22, 23 and 24. In the first of these David in his great need cries to God as his Saviour, in whom he puts his trust:

> *"You are enthroned as the Holy One;*
> *You are the praise of Israel.*
> *In you our fathers put their trust;*

Psalms

> *They trusted and you delivered them.*
> *They cried to you and were saved;*
> *In you they trusted and were not disappointed."*
> *(Psalm 22:3-5)*

As his Saviour, David can look to God as his shepherd in Psalm 23 who is with him through all the circumstances of life:

> *"The LORD is my shepherd, I shall not be in want.*
> *He makes me lie down in green pastures."*
> *(Psalm 23:1-2)*

Because David has known his salvation and his leading he can look forward to God as his coming King, the King of glory:

> *"Lift up your heads, O you gates;*
> *be lifted up, you ancient doors,*
> *that the King of glory may come in.*
> *Who is this King of glory?*
> *The LORD strong and mighty,*
> *the LORD mighty in battle."*
> *(Psalm 24:7-8)*

Here in these three psalms we see how David is pointing forward to the role of Jesus in the New Testament; how He must first be our Saviour before becoming our Shepherd who leads us to anticipate His second coming as 'King of glory'.

Other psalms are written for special occasions which were intended for those making pilgrimage to Jerusalem. Psalms 113-118 are psalms sung at Passover. Psalms 146-150 are 'Hallelujah' or 'Praise the LORD for festivals of rejoicing.

Then there are psalms to express particular emotions such as the Lamont psalms written out of personal unhappiness. In these we find a lot of self-pity expressed but these feelings are put before God and healing is found.

> *"O LORD God Almighty,*
> *will your anger smoulder*
> *against the prayers of your people?*
> *You have fed them with the bread of tears;*
> *you have made them drink tears by the bowlful.*
> *You have made us an object of derision*
> *to our neighbours,*
> *and our enemies mock us.*
> *Restore us, God Almighty;*
> *Make your face shine upon us,*
> *that we may be saved."*
> *(Psalm 80:4-7)*

In contrast with these, we have the psalms of gratitude in which flow a proclamation of praise.

> *"Your love, O LORD, reaches to the heavens,*
> *your faithfulness to the skies.*
> *Your righteousness is like the highest mountains,*
> *your justice like the great deep.*
> *You LORD, preserve both people and animals.*
> *How priceless is your unfailing love, O God!"*
> *(Psalm 36:5-7)*

Perhaps the emotion expressed that we find hardest to accept is that of vengeance on their enemies. Psalm 140:9-11 and Psalm 137:8-9 are very unpleasant for there is no forgiveness for their enemies:

> *"Daughter Babylon, doomed to destruction,*
> *happy is the one who repays you*
> *according to what you have done to us.-*

Psalms

> *Happy is the one who seizes your infants*
> *and dashes them against the rocks."*
> *(Psalm 137:8-9)*

The psalmist is honestly expressing his feelings to God and was not suggesting that he should practise such vengeance. The psalm quoted in particular was written on behalf of the nation and was not personal. These people had not received the teaching of Jesus concerning our treatment of our enemies, nor did they know about the Day of Judgement, heaven and hell. They prayed to God to be vindicated in this life.

In the psalms we have a very detailed view of God. We are told of His transcendence, that is, He is beyond our understanding and of His immanence, that is, He is here with us, close to us. We are encouraged to magnify Him; not because we can make Him bigger, but so that our view of Him may be enlarged. The psalmists frequently tell of His attributes, for instance:

> *"the Lord is compassionate and gracious,*
> *slow to anger, abounding in love.*
> *He will not always accuse,*
> *nor will he harbour his anger for ever;*
> *he does not treat us as our sins deserve*
> *or repay us according to our iniquities.*
> *For as high as the heavens are above the earth,*
> *so great is his love for those who fear him."*
> *(Psalm 103:8-11)*

In Psalm 139, David describes how omnipotent (all-powerful), omniscient (all-knowing) and omnipresent (everywhere) He is. We also learn in the psalms of the actions or the Lord, as in Psalm 33:

Psalms

*"By the word of the L*ORD *the heavens were made
their starry host by the breath of his mouth.
He gathers the waters of the sea into jars,
He puts the deep into storehouses.
Let all the earth fear the L*ORD*;
let all the people of the world revere Him.
For He spoke and it came to be;
 he commanded, and it stood firm.
The L*ORD *foils the plans of the nations;
He thwarts the purposes of the peoples.
but the plans of the L*ORD *stand firm forever,
The purposes of His heart through all generations."
(Psalm 33:6-11)*

The psalmists introduce us to our God as our Shepherd, Warrior, Judge, Father, and above all as our Saviour and King. Certainly in the psalms we find the God of loving concern for His people, whom Jesus came to reveal to us more fully in the New Testament. Indeed much of the life of Jesus as the Messiah or Christ is prophesied by the psalmists.

Proverbs,

In Proverbs we have the author, King Solomon, a middle-aged father, desperately trying to prevent a young man from making bad choices in his life. He presents his son, and his readers, with the alternatives that life offers, and how they will affect him. Does he want wisdom or folly as his companion for life? He symbolically portrays both these options as women.

Solomon expresses his advice in the form of proverbs, a short familiar saying which proclaims a truth. These are intended as guidelines not as guarantees of promises from God. They describe life as it really is, not life in the House of God, but life in the street, the office, the school, the shop, the home, thus covering all aspects of life.

Proverbs consider how you should live life throughout the week in every situation. In order to press home his point of view, Solomon frequently uses antithesis – wisdom versus folly, righteousness versus wickedness, good versus evil, wealth versus poverty, honour versus dishonour, permanence versus transience, truth versus falsehood, industry versus indolence, friend versus enemy, prudence versus rashness, fidelity versus adultery, peace versus violence, life versus death.

The proverbs tell us how we can make the most of life and warn us that many people waste it.

In his prologue to this book, Solomon states that to embrace wisdom is the only way to lead a satisfactory life.

"The fear of the LORD is the beginning of knowledge but fools despise wisdom and instruction." (Proverbs 1:7)

Proverbs

Solomon affirms the truth that God is the All-Wise God, the source of all wisdom and that it is His wisdom that created the whole universe, with all its complexity.

If we learn from Proverbs we will understand that to 'fear God' is the first step in gaining wisdom. We must seek Him for wisdom so that we can handle the affairs of the world in a shrewd and sound way. God uses other people, too, to pass on wisdom to us, especially parents and grandparents and other people more experienced than us.

To enjoy God's wisdom, we must be obedient to do what He tells us to do.

In Chapters 8 and 9 we are given a detailed description of the lady 'Wisdom' how she appeals to mankind to listen to her and follow her ways:

> *"Listen for I have worthy things to say;*
> *I open my lips to speak what is right.*
> *my mouth speaks what is true,*
> *For my lips detest wickedness.*
> *Choose my instructions instead of silver,*
> *Knowledge rather than choice gold,*
> *for wisdom is more precious than rubies,*
> *and nothing you desire can compare with her."*
> *(Proverbs 8:6-7; 10-11.)*

In Chapter 31 we see wisdom as the ideal wife. Whereas the woman 'folly' is depicted as a prostitute, who seduces her victims and leads them to their death.

> *"With persuasive words she led him astray, he*
> *seduced him with her smooth talk.*
> *All at once he followed her*
> *like an ox going to the slaughter,*

Like a deer stepping into a noose
till an arrow pierces his liver,
Like a bird darting into a snare,
little knowing it will cost him his life."
(Proverbs 7:21-23)

Solomon sees wisdom and folly as moral choices, rather than mental ones. Someone can be mentally clever and morally foolish.

A wise man is able to discern between good and evil; he knows how to respond to and deal with any given situation. He is discreet and realistic, with power to make plans. He is open to correction and reproof, keen to turn away from his own independence and self-reliance to submit to God. Instead of fearing men, he fears God, valuing His truth at any price.

A fool is described as ignorant, obstinate, arrogant, perverted, boring, aimless, irresponsible, gullible, careless, complacent, insolent, sullen, and argumentative. He wants everything on a plate, does not think for himself, prefers fantasy to fact, illusions to truth. At best he is disturbing, at worst he is dangerous. He is a sorrow to his parents, yet he despises them as old-fashioned.

There is much advice about relationships in 'Proverbs', both in the family and between friends. Solomon sees the family unit as the pivot of society. Parents have the responsibility for training and disciplining their children, for foolishness is bound up in the heart of a child, so they need encouragement to be wise. However, they are free to welcome or despise the instructions they are given. Another key subject is the tongue and the sins of speech, for what is in the heart comes out of the mouth.

Proverbs

*"A gentle answer turns away wrath,
but a harsh word stirs up anger.
The tongue of the wise adorns knowledge,
but the mouth of the fool gushes folly."
(Proverbs 15:1-2)*

There are four categories of words that should be on our lips, honest words, few words, calm words and apt words.

Solomon was also concerned that the advice given in this book needed to be followed by those governing the nation of Israel. He knew that 'Righteousness exalts a nation' and that if Israel did not live by God's truth as expressed here, then they were heading for disaster. Only a loving God would care so much for His people that having given them freewill, He then took great pains to guide them to make wise choices.

Ecclesiastes

Solomon wrote 'Ecclesiastes' in his old age when he was very disillusioned, disappointed and hopeless. It is a very unusual book for it is written as if the author was having a debate within his own mind and the book is the outcome, in which he expressed both sides of the debate. The subjects up for debate are, 'What is life about? Is life worth living? How can we make the most of life?'

Throughout the book he switches from one side to the other; on the one hand he expresses the view of the worldly man, and on the other, the view of the man whose heart is set on God.

In his opening statement, Solomon speaks of his utter disillusionment with all that he has at the end of a long life. He was a very wealthy King who had been given much wisdom which he used to engage in a vast number of activities to find satisfaction and happiness.

"I, the Teacher, was king over Israel in Jerusalem. I applied my mind to study and to explore by wisdom all that is done under the heavens." (Ecclesiastes 1:12-13).

However, there were limitations to his search, everything was 'under the sun'. That is, he did not look beyond the confines of this earth. His other limitation was that of time.

"Then I said to myself,
The fate of the fool will overtake me also.
What then do I gain by being wise?
I said to myself.
'This too is meaningless.'
for the wise, like the fool will not
be long remembered;

Ecclesiastes

*the days have already come when both
 have been forgotten
Like the fool, the wise man too must die!"
(Ecclesiastes 2:15-16)*

He seemed only aware of fulfilment whilst on the earth. 'While we are still alive.' There is no indication that he considered a life after death. He assumed there was no loving God, neither heaven nor hell.

Then in Chapter 3 he resigns himself to God's pattern for existence; everything has its set time.

"There is a time for everything, and a season for every activity under heaven: a time to be born and a time to die, a time to plant and a time to uproot." (Ecclesiastes 3:1-2)

It is God's world which He created perfect.

"I know everything God does will endure forever; nothing can be added to it and nothing taken from it. God does it so that men will revere Him." (Ecclesiastes 3:14).

When Solomon does think of God:

*"I said to myself,
God will bring into judgement
both the righteous and the wicked
for there will be a time for every activity,
a time to judge every deed."
(Ecclesiastes 3:17)*

There is a lifting of his pessimism. However, this sullen mood again takes hold of him as he considers all the oppression, toil and friendlessness in this world. Wealth does not give satisfaction; the more you have the more you want and yet

> *"but as for the rich, their abundance*
> *permits them no sleep," (Ecclesiastes 5:12).*

He even finds his gift from God of wisdom, a burden:

> *"Do not be over-righteous,*
> *neither be over wise –*
> *why destroy yourself?"*
> *(Ecclesiastes 7:16)*

In his despair, he looks again to God:

> *"Whoever fears God will avoid all extremes."*
> *(Ecclesiastes 7:18)*

His advice to the young man:

> *"Remember your Creator*
> *in the days of your youth,*
> *before the days of trouble come."*
> *(Ecclesiastes 12:1)*

He knew that the relationship he had with God in his youth was forgotten in his pursuit of the knowledge of all that there was to know in the world.

His final advice:

> *"Now all has been heard;*
> *here is the conclusion of the matter;*
> *fear God and keep his commandments,*
> *for this is the duty of all mankind.*
> *For God will bring every deed into judgement,*
> *including every hidden thing,*

whether it is good or evil."
(Ecclesiastes 12:13-14)

He knew that if true justice is lacking on this earth, there would come a day when mankind would meet their maker and receive true justice from Him.

In this strange book we are left in no doubt that those who turn their backs on God and go their own way, seeking to find meaning to life from work, wealth, leisure activities, family and friends rarely find all that they were hoping for, a happy, contented life.

Song of Solomon

In the 'Song of Songs', which is referred to in the first verse, as Solomon's Song of Songs, we have a romantic story of a young couple meeting and falling in love.

As the story develops we see how their love grows to the point where he proposes to her and she eagerly accepts. No sooner have they become engaged than he has to leave her to attend to his business elsewhere. While he is away she has nightmares, dreading that he will not return and she will never see him again.

However one day she is told that the King is coming to visit his estate which is where she lives. When the King in his carriage comes in sight, she is shocked to find he is the young man who has proposed marriage to her. It is well-known that he already has many wives. Nevertheless he seeks her out again to be his bride and to take her back to his palace.

She goes south with him and is married in Jerusalem. At the wedding banquet, even though she sits next to the King, she feels very inferior to all his other beautiful wives. She speaks of herself to her husband as a rose of Sharon, a very insignificant wild flower. However, he assures her that to him she is 'a lily among thorns'; the lily is the most beautiful flower in Israel. This sets her heart at rest.

What has this love story to do with understanding more clearly about our Father God? I believe this book was included in the Old Testament, even though there is no mention of God in it, because it can be seen as an analogy, a parallelism, with God's love for His people. God did not intend for His people Israel to have just another religion in which they were rewarded for being obedient. He wanted a personal relationship with them; for them to know Him as King David

Song of Solomon

did. As David trusted His God for his very life when facing the bear and the lion, he fell in love with Him and expressed that love in the psalms he wrote.

This love relationship is what God seeks from all His subjects, Jew and Christian. It is a deeply emotional relationship even as the lover has toward his beloved.

> *"How delightful is your love, my sister, my bride!*
> *How much more pleasing is your love than wine,*
> *and the fragrance of your perfume*
> *more than any spice."*
> *(Song of Songs 4:10)*

It is not a secret love affair to be kept hidden, but has to be openly declared. Solomon took his beloved to Jerusalem to be his bride, for all to see. So too, the Israelites were to declare their love relationship with their God to all the nations around them.

Isaiah

This book covers the visions concerning Judah and Jerusalem that Isaiah (the prophet) the son of Amoz saw.

Chapter one has a summary of Isaiah's message; a condensed version of Chapters 1-39. The perfect Father has done everything for His children yet their response to His loving care was even worse than would be expected of a dumb brute.

> *"The ox knows his master,*
> *the donkey his owner's manger,*
> *but Israel does not know,*
> *my people do not understand."*
> *(Isaiah 1:3)*

Despite the fact that they are incurably religious for there is no shortage of sacrifices or feasts, they have forsaken, despised and are estranged from their God. Their religion does not evoke godliness in them.

They worship with all the right ritual, but there is no righteousness in their hearts. God looks at their hearts and if these are not right, He will not listen to their prayers.

> *"When you spread out your hands in prayer,*
> *I hide my eyes from you;*
> *even when you offer many prayers,*
> *I will not listen.*
> *Your hands are full of blood!"*
> *(Isaiah 1:15)*

In the temple, had God been blessed and glorified? God

Isaiah

wants repentance; for them to cease doing evil and learn to do good. They must put right what is wrong.

The prophets sometimes are writing or speaking of the present state of affairs as Isaiah does in chapter one, and at other times their prophecy looks into the future. We see this at the beginning of the second chapter in which Isaiah brings the good news of the last days to bring hope and comfort to the people who have fallen under condemnation and judgement because of the folly of their present way of life.

They were putting their trust in superstition, money, military power and idols, but God can and will bring all these false hopes down to the ground, in order to humble them and bring them to their senses.

However having given these stark warnings chapter four ends with a prophecy of future encouragement; the coming of a Messiah who will be the pride and glory of Israel. He will bring two things, individual purity – the survivors of Israel shall each be called holy, and a return to the days of the wilderness when God protected His people.

Isaiah has a new approach in chapter 5. To draw the people's attention, he sings them a love song, words and music given by the Holy Spirit. It was a song of a woman who sings of her lover who owns a vineyard. This vineyard was given great care and attention but it only yielded bad fruit; nothing good grew in it. What was he to do?

Isaiah was hoping to get his fellow countrymen on his side mentally before he challenged them morally.

The song continues with the owner breaking up his vineyard. Then he comes clean:

Isaiah

> *"The vineyard of the* L<small>ORD</small> *Almighty*
> *is the nation of Israel,*
> *and the people of Judah*
> *are the vines he delighted in.*
> *And He looked for justice,*
> *but saw bloodshed;*
> *for righteousness,*
> *but heard cries of distress."*
> *(Isaiah 5:7)*

What more could a God who is wholly love do to cure this world of sin? He must deal with the 'wild grapes' which He does by putting a curse on them,

> *"Woe (curse) to those who call evil good*
> *and good evil,*
> *who put darkness for light*
> *and light for darkness,*
> *who put bitter for sweet*
> *and sweet for bitter."*
> *(Isaiah 5:20)*

In chapter 6 we have Isaiah's vision of God's holiness and his call. You cannot love God until you have seen that He is holy. We only experience God's love through forgiveness.

> *"Woe to me!" I cried. "I am ruined! For I am a man of unclean lips, and I live among a people of unclean lips, and my eyes have seen the King, the* L<small>ORD</small> *Almighty. Then one of the seraphs flew to me with a live coal in his hand, which he had taken with tongs from the altar. With it he touched my mouth and said, "See, this has touched your lips; your guilt is taken away and your sin atoned for." (Isaiah 6:5-7).*

After this cleansing experience, Isaiah felt able to answer God's call to be His prophet in the affirmative. God made it clear to him that it was no easy task; people would listen but not understand. They would look but never see the point. In fact his preaching would make them worse, but still God wanted him to preach.

Although Isaiah died without appreciation, now his words are very precious to millions of people the world over.

Israel's relationship with her God had gone wrong when she engaged in too much political activity as seen in chapters 7 and 8. The key word in these chapters is 'fear' or 'dread' – a wrong emotion for the people of God. It reveals that they had got out of touch with Him. God was angry because of their pride and self-sufficiency; they were living as if He did not exist. Selfishness and injustice was widespread; widows and orphans were exploited. For all this, their heavenly Father's hand had to punish. Isaiah uses the refrain,

> "Yet for all this, His anger is not turned away,
> his hand is still upraised."
> (Isaiah 9:12)

Assyria was the instrument in God's hand; He allowed them to invade Israel to bring the people to their senses. The threat of losing what was precious to them made them wake up; it certainly brought Judah to her senses.

We learn so much about God in these chapters. Firstly that He can be very angry; that He is provoked to anger by acts of unrighteousness. Secondly that He is a very powerful God who has His hand on the pulse of history; it is He who controls the nations and will use an aggressor as a means of punishment, but only so far – a warning is given which if taken, causes a withdrawal but when ignored, then the punishment in full follows.

Isaiah

However through it all God loves His children, and will not let them go, but saves a remnant to fulfil His purposes. There are eleven chapters devoted to the geography and history of the region. God fixes His truth in time and place; facts which can be checked upon from other sources. This gives the whole book a solid foundation.

In these chapters we see that when Judah was in trouble she was greatly tempted to ally herself with other nations without a thought as to what God's will on the matter might be. Isaiah, though, warned them that their first move should be to approach God through prayer and seek His wisdom; a lesson they learnt the hard way. Their pride made them feel they could manage without God. When disaster struck and they were exiled and humbled, they found their way back to their Father God and learnt the truth of Isaiah's promise.

> *"You will keep in perfect peace*
> *Those whose minds are steadfast,*
> *because they trust in you.*
> *Trust in the LORD forever,*
> *for the LORD, the LORD himself, is the Rock eternal.*
> *He humbles those who dwell on high,*
> *he lays the lofty city low."*
> *(Isaiah 26:3-5a)*

In this book, God not only gives Isaiah many warnings for Israel, Judah and the nations surrounding them, but also for the whole earth. Chapter 24 contains a very dire warning concerning God's judgement of the whole earth.

> *"The earth will be completely laid waste*
> *and totally plundered.*
> *The LORD has spoken this word.*
> *Therefore a curse consumes the earth;*
> *its people must bear their guilt.*

Isaiah

Therefore earth's inhabitants are burned up,
and very few are left. In that day (the day of
judgement) the LORD
will punish
the powers in the heavens above
and the kings on the earth below."
(Isaiah 24:3, 6, 21)

This is not the end for those who are faithful and true to Him. There is a new heaven and a new earth in which God will meet with His people and feast with them.

"He will swallow up death forever.
The Sovereign LORD will wipe away the tears
from all faces;
Surely this is our God;
we trusted in Him and He saved us.
This is the LORD, we trusted in him;
let us rejoice and be glad in his salvation."
(Isaiah 25:8a-9)

Chapters 28 to 33 are sermons of Isaiah in which he spoke of God's woes or curses on ungodliness; curse on drunkenness, on Jerusalem for its ritualistic religion, on their obstinacy, on their reliance on foreign allies and on those who destroy and betray. In each chapter Isaiah speaks of how God's justice will punish their behaviour; however there will always be a remnant who will receive His goodness. Such teaching was scoffed at; Isaiah was accused of treating them like children. When the punishment (exile) came, they saw how true, the word given was.

Despite all the warnings to the contrary, His 'obstinate children' made alliances with Egypt. This was to lead to their downfall, though the Lord longed for it to be otherwise.

Isaiah

The Lord said,

> *"In repentance and rest is your salvation, quietness and trust is your strength, but you would have none of it.*
> *Yet the LORD longs to be gracious to you;*
> *therefore he will rise up to show you compassion.*
> *For the LORD is a God of justice.*
> *Blessed are all who wait for him."*
> *(Isaiah 30:15 & 18)*

The promise again is when God has dealt with the obstinate, He will raise up a righteous king who will rule with justice.

> *"See, a king will reign in righteousness*
> *and rulers will rule with justice.*
> *Each man will be like a shelter from the wind*
> *and a refuge from the storm,*
> *like streams of water in the desert*
> *and the shadow of a great rock in a thirsty land.*
> *Then the eyes of those who see will no longer be closed,*
> *and the ears of those who hear will listen."*
> *(Isaiah 32:1-3)*

Chapter 34 returns to the judgement of the nations who have fought against God's people

> *"For the LORD has a day of vengeance,*
> *a year of retribution, to uphold Zion's cause."*
> *(Isaiah 34:8)*

The following chapter tells of the joy of those who have repented and been redeemed.

Isaiah

"and those the LORD *has rescued will return.*
They will enter Zion with singing; everlasting joy will crown their heads,
Gladness and joy will overtake them,
and sorrow and signing will flee away."
(Isaiah 35:10)

Chapters 36 to 39 relate the history of the Assyrian attack on Judah; King Hezekiah's prayer to God on this occasion and God's salvation of the nation.

The final twenty-seven chapters of Isaiah, 40-66, have a completely different atmosphere from the first thirty-nine chapters, even as the Old Testament has from the New Testament. In the first part of the book, Isaiah hammered home the judgement of God because of Israel's idolatry and injustice.

However, Chapter 40 begins with the word, "comfort" which is the theme for the rest of the book. 'Comfort' in this context means, 'with strength', that is, to comfort someone is to put strength into their soul. These twenty-seven chapters are to build up the people of God; to strengthen them and make them hopeful, rejoicing and confident. Whereas in the first half of the book, God's righteousness was the cause of His punishment of His people, in the second half, His righteousness led to His saving His people from their enemies.

The background to this section is 150 years later. The Israelites had received the punishment of exile that Isaiah had warned them about; for 70 long years they suffered in Babylon. It was during this time that the latter part of Isaiah's prophecy was made known to them. The Holy Spirit had shown him that in their suffering, Israel would come to appreciate their God; His love for them and His promise to save and redeem them.

Isaiah

Isaiah seeks to magnify their vision of their God;

> *"To whom will you compare me?*
> *Or who is my equal?" says the Holy One.*
> *"Life your eyes and look to the heavens;*
> *who created all these?"*
> *(Isaiah 40:25, 26)*

They were to see that God was far greater than their problems. They had thought God has forgotten them, and complained. Isaiah reminds them that those who put their hope in God, God will strengthen, enabling them to push through their present circumstances. He also warns the Babylonians that He will use His strength against them. The God of Israel was the God of History and would raise up a pagan king, Cyrus, King of the Persians to defeat the Babylonians, and free the Israelites to return to their own land.

> *"So do not fear, for I am with you,*
> *do not be dismayed, for I am your God.*
> *I will strengthen you and help you.*
> *I will uphold you with my righteous right hand."*
> *(Isaiah 41:10)*

God had intended for 'His chosen people', the Israelites, to serve Him by being obedient to His commandments and doing His will. In these chapters He refers to His people often as

> *"But you, O Israel, my Servant,*
> *Jacob, whom I have chosen,*
> *you descendants of Abraham my friend,*
> *I took you from the ends of the earth,*
> *from its farthest corners I called you.*
> *I said, 'You are my servant';*
> *I have chosen you and have not rejected you."*
> *(Isaiah 41:8-9)*

Isaiah

However despite the loving care lavished upon them, the Israelites miserably failed to be the servant God was looking for:

> *"If only you had paid attention to my commands*
> *your peace would have been like a river.*
> *your well-being like the waves of the sea.*
> *Your descendants would have been like the sand,*
> *your children like its numberless grains."*
> *(Isaiah 48:18-19)*

And so God's promise was to send a Messiah into their midst, Jesus, the Son of God. He is predestined by God, the Father to do the work that Israel had failed to do; to be His servant; that through Him, the world would come to know the Israelite God as the one who would save them from their sins. Although this Messiah was of the lineage of King David and as such had a right to the throne of Israel, Isaiah warns that when He came He would be far different from their expectations.

> *"He grew up before him like a tender shoot,*
> *and like a root out of dry ground.*
> *He had no beauty or majesty to attract us to him."*
> *(Isaiah 53:2b)*

Note that, although written 750 years before Jesus lived on earth, Isaiah includes himself as one of those who did not recognise Him as Messiah. This suggests that it was not just the Jews of His day who would fail to acknowledge Him, but that His rejection would be more universal. The most important message of Chapter 53 is that Father God, to demonstrate His great love for mankind, would allow His Son to suffer and die ignominiously. He was to be the sacrifice for all time; the perfect, sinless man to be offered for the sins of mankind.

> *"But he was pierced for our transgressions,*
> *he was crushed for our iniquities;*
> *the punishment that bought us peace was upon Him,*
> *and by his wounds we are healed.*
> *We all, like sheep, have gone astray,*
> *each of us has turned to his own way;*
> *and the LORD has laid on him*
> *the iniquity of us all."*
> *(Isaiah 53:5 & 6)*

This was a punishment for a crime for which He could not truly be found guilty.

Chapter 53 is the climax of the whole book and in the following chapters, having given his people a reason to rejoice, Isaiah returns to the circumstances in which they would find themselves, after exile in Babylon. He sees Jerusalem as a barren woman whose desire for children would be fulfilled.

> *"Enlarge the place of your tent,*
> *stretch your tent curtains wide,*
> *do not hold back;*
> *lengthen your cords,*
> *strengthen your stakes.*
> *For you will spread out to the right and to the left;*
> *your descendants will dispossess nations*
> *and settle in their desolate cities."*
> *(Isaiah 54:2 & 3)*

There are many promises that he makes concerning the well-being of the nation.

> *"For your Maker is your husband –*
> *The LORD Almighty is His name*
> *All your children will be taught by the LORD,*

*and great will be your children's peace and you will
refute every tongue that accuses you."
(Isaiah 54:5b,13,17a)*

They must, as always, listen to what God has to tell them.

*"Seek the LORD, while He may be found;
Call on Him while He is near.
Let the wicked forsake His way
And the evil man his thoughts."
(Isaiah 55:6-7)*

Also they must have a far greater view of their God.

*"For my thoughts are not your thoughts,
Neither your ways my ways,"
declares the LORD.
"As the heavens are higher than the earth,
so are my ways higher than your ways,
and my thoughts than your thoughts."
(Isaiah 55:8-9)*

During their history of being God's chosen people, the Jews felt for the most part, that God was especially theirs. They made no effort to spread their faith, outside of their nation. However in Chapter 56 Isaiah speaks of God having a relationship with foreigners.

*"And foreigners who bind themselves to the LORD to
minister to him,
to love the name of the LORD,
and to be his servants,
all who keep the Sabbath without desecrating it
and who hold fast to my covenant –
these I will bring to my holy mountain
and give them joy in my house of prayer."*

(Isaiah 56:6-7)

These who serve Him will have preference over those of Israel who have turned their back on Him. The wicked with whom God will have no relationship, are defined in more detail in Chapter 57.

Whilst in exile the Jews were denied sacrifices, having no temple, but they did seek to worship God with prayer and fasting. Despite praying daily and fasting frequently, often in sackcloth, they were frustrated by the lack of answers from God. Did He not care? Isaiah gives the reason for His apparent indifference to their worship in Chapter 58.

What they had considered to be their good behaviour, spending time in prayer and fasting, God was not satisfied with. Such worship was apart from the rest of their lives and had no reference to how they lived for the rest of the week.

> *"For day after day they seek me out;*
> *they seem eager to know my ways,*
> *as if they were a nation that does what is right*
> *and has not forsaken the commands of its God.*
> *They ask me for just decisions*
> *And seem eager for God to come near them.*
> *'Why have we fasted', they say,*
> *'and you have not seen it?*
> *Why have we humbled ourselves,*
> *and you have not noticed?"*
> *(Isaiah 58:2-3)*

Isaiah points out to them that even when they had met for prayer and were fasting, they still carried on business as usual and exploited their employees. God demanded a complete giving up of self and selfish ways, "to loosen the chains of injustice"; rather than just deny their bodies' food.

Isaiah

> *"Is it not to share your food with the hungry
> and to provide the poor wanderer with shelter –
> when you see the naked, to clothe him,
> and not to turn away from your own flesh and
> blood?"*
> *(Isaiah 58:7)*

> *"Then you will call, and the LORD will answer;
> you will cry for help and he will say;
> here I am'."*
> *(Isaiah 58:9)*

In the next chapter, Isaiah deals with their wicked ways which keep them from God.

> *"Surely the arm of the LORD is not too short to save,
> nor his ear too dull to hear.
> But your iniquities have separated you from your
> God."*
> *(Isaiah 59:1-2)*

A just God cannot ignore these evil deeds.

The final six chapters of the prophecy give us a glimpse into the future. The realisation that God has planned a life for His people beyond this life on earth, has been a mainstay of hope throughout the ages. In Chapters 60 to 62 we read of His establishing a new Jerusalem, as the centre of civilisation, the capital of the universe; God says to Jerusalem, here called Zion.

> *"See, darkness covers the earth
> and thick darkness is over the peoples,
> but the LORD rises upon you
> and his glory appears over you.
> Nations will come to your light,
> and kings to the brightness of your dawn."*

(Isaiah 60:1-2)

The nations will come with their wealth ready to help build up the walls.

In the next chapter, Isaiah promises that God will meet every need of His people living in Zion.

> *"To bestow on them a crown of beauty*
> *instead of ashes*
> *The oil of gladness instead of mourning,*
> *and a garment of praise*
> *instead of a spirit of despair "*
> *(Isaiah 61:3)*
>
> *"And you will be called priests of the LORD.*
> *You will be named ministers of our God.*
> *You will feed on the wealth of nations,*
> *and in their riches you will boast."*
> *(Isaiah 61: 6)*

Not only the inhabitants but also the city itself will have a completely new face lift

> *"The nations will see your vindication,*
> *and all kings your glory;*
> *you will be called by a new name*
> *that the mouth of the LORD will bestow.*
> *You will be a crown of splendour in the LORD'S hand,*
> *A royal diadem in the hand of your God."*
> *(Isaiah 62:2-3)*

The next vision that Isaiah has, is of someone coming towards Jerusalem, covered in red, which Isaiah takes to be wine juice and that he has come from the winepress (Hebrew Bozrah) in Edom. When he questions Him, he discovers that in fact it is blood, the blood of vengeance. This is in fact, a vision of the 'Day of Judgement' on which all mankind come to face Jesus and hear His verdict on their life on earth. Those whose sins have not been forgiven will be wiped out.

> *"I trampled the nations in my anger;*
> *in my wrath I made them drunk*
> *and poured their blood on the ground."*
> *(Isaiah 63:6)*

This was too much for Isaiah to accept and he immediately recalls the goodness of God and His great love. How could a God of love bring such retribution upon the people He created, especially upon the people He had chosen for Himself?

There follows an impassioned prayer of Isaiah's in which he cries to God to look down from heaven and have compassion on His people; all have sinned. Why did God not stop them? In his fervour, Isaiah appeals to God to rend the heavens and come down and do something to stop the sinning.

> *"We are the clay, you are the potter;*
> *we are all the work of your hand.*
> *Do not be angry, beyond measure, LORD;*
> *do not remember our sins forever."*
> *(Isaiah 64:8-9)*

Chapter 65 begins with the answer to this prayer. God did come down and reveal Himself.

> *"All day long I have held out my hands*
> *to an obstinate people,*
> *Who walk in ways not good,*
> *pursuing their own imaginations –*

Isaiah

> *a people who continually provoke me to my very face,*
> *offering sacrifices in gardens*
> *and burning incense on altars of brick."*
> *(Isaiah 65:2-3)*

He has done His best to draw His people unto Himself.

> *"for I called but you did not answer,*
> *I spoke but you did not listen.*
> *You did evil in my sight*
> *and chose what displeases me."*
> *(Isaiah 65:12b)*

Those who did accept Him, who were willing to serve Him, will be rewarded. Those who have rebelled against Him, have no place in the new heaven and new earth; they have devised their own religion to defend themselves against God. It is a vision of the new heaven and new earth that God opens up before us at the end of the chapter.

> *"The wolf and the lamb will feed together,*
> *and the lion will eat straw like the ox,*
> *and dust will be the serpent's food.*
> *They will neither harm nor destroy.*
> *on all my holy mountain,'*
> *says the LORD."*
> *(Isaiah 65:25)*

The final chapter comes back to the exiles and their return to Jerusalem with the intention of rebuilding the temple. God reminds them that no temple would ever be able to house Him.

> *"This is what the LORD says:*
> *'Heaven is my throne,*
> *and the earth is my footstall.*

Isaiah

Where is the house you will build for me?
Where will my resting place be?
Has not my hand made all these things,
and so they came into being?" declares the LORD.
(Isaiah 66:1-2)

He is more concerned about His Spirit living within each person so that they are humble before Him. The rites of worship offered in the temple have no significance to God if for the rest of the week, the worshipper turns his back on God and seeks his own pleasures.

"They have chosen their own ways
And they delight in their abominations."
(Isaiah 66:3b)

God made it clear to them that they could not guarantee His presence just by putting up a building; it has to have the right kind of people inside; those 'who tremble at His word'. God wanted all their time, space and energy.

God then promises that though they would return to a devastated city, Jerusalem would very quickly come to life again. The people in this restored city must themselves be restored to fulfil the purpose God had for them; only a remnant would survive to do this.

"They will proclaim my glory among the nations, and they will bring all your people from all the nations to my holy mountain in Jerusalem as an offering to the LORD."
(Isaiah 66:19b-20)

Jeremiah

Jeremiah's forty year prophetic career covered the reigns of the last five kings of Judah. He spoke at a traumatic time for the people of God. The ten tribes of the Northern Kingdom had been taken into exile by Assyria; Isaiah was dead and his message largely unheeded. Jeremiah had to warn the Kingdom of Judah that it was almost too late to stop disaster coming.

God often gave Jeremiah His message to the people through the means of visions. One such vision was of a potter working on a lump of clay to make a vessel. God was showing His relationship to His people. His intention was to make something beautiful with His people, but if they remained like the clay hard and unresistant – which was their prerogative for God had given them a free will, He could only form an ugly shape.

God is not dealing with puppets and decreeing what they should be. Rather, even at this late stage, He wanted a response from them, so that He could make them, with their co-operation, what He wanted. However the vision has something further to say the ugly pot was baked and taken to the valley where rubbish was thrown and broken into pieces. God would allow His people to be broken.

Jeremiah's basic message was very similar to that of Isaiah; God pulls down those who disobey Him and builds up those who obey. His life as a prophet was exceedingly tough for he was in the thick of the political world in Jerusalem, but God enabled him to push through all the adversity which his message engendered toward his person. Although he was a speaker, most of his speaking was in poetic form, as he was

Jeremiah

communicating God's 'heart language' that is His feelings. This is a very emotional book.

Jeremiah allowed God complete control of his life. Often his message was conveyed by the way he lived. When everyone in Jerusalem was trying to sell their property because they knew when the Babylonians came it would be worthless, God told Jeremiah to buy property. He invested in a field to demonstrate that God would keep His word and bring them back to their land.

Most of his prophecy like Isaiah's is taken up with revealing the sins of the nation. He expresses God's regret and anger, but in that there are mixed emotions for God truly loves the people of Israel but cannot let them go on as they are.

> *"Your own conduct and actions*
> *have brought this upon you.*
> *How bitter it is!*
> *How it pierces to the heart!*
> *Oh, My anguish, My anguish!*
> *I writhe in pain.*
> *Oh, the agony of my heart!*
> *My heart pounds within me,*
> *I cannot keep silent.*
> *For I have heard the sound of the trumpet;*
> *I have heard the battle cry.*
> *Disaster follows disaster;*
> *the whole land lies in ruins.*
> *In an instant my tents are destroyed,*
> *my shelter in a moment.*
> *How long must I see the battle standard*
> *and hear the sound of the trumpet?*
> *My people are fools;*
> *they do not know Me.*

Jeremiah

They are senseless children;
they have no understanding.
They are skilled in doing evil;
they know not how to do good."
(Jeremiah 4:18-22)

The people have been led astray by their leaders. God lays the blame on the corrupt prophets, priests and kings.

"Both prophet and priest are godless;
even in my Temple I find their wickedness" declares
the LORD
(Jeremiah 23:11)

There were many false prophets who made claim to dreams and visions which suggested all would be well; that Jeremiah was lying to them.

The priests too, were giving the people false hope by stating that God's Temple was so holy that God would not allow any nation to harm it. If the people attended services in the Temple, the very act of ceremonial worship was enough to keep them in God's good books and ensure His protection.

"Will you steal and murder, commit adultery and perjury, burn incense to Baal and follow other gods you have not known, and then come and stand before me in this house, which bears my Name, and say, 'We are safe'– safe to do all these detestable things? Has this house, which bears my Name, become a den of robbers to you? But I have been watching!" declares the LORD.' (Jeremiah 7:9-11)

Jeremiah declares the need for worship to be a spiritual act, and that religious ritual was useless if the heart was not in it. He emphasises the need for the people to praise God,

Jeremiah

pray and read the Scriptures when they met together. In this way, he prepared them for their time in exile when there would be no temple, nor sacrifices and yet they could still have a relationship with their God.

None of the last five kings of Judah lived lives which were an example of holy living to their subjects. All were involved in evil practices and failed to uphold justice in the land. They, too, had false hopes of security in that they were of the line of David. Jeremiah's warnings of how the Lord would deal with them, was met with contempt.

Jeremiah loved his nation and so wanted to make a positive impact upon them to keep the people together where God had planted them.

> *"we acknowledge our wickedness, LORD,*
> *And the guilt of our ancestors;*
> *we have indeed sinned against you.*
> *For the sake of your name do not despise us;*
> *do not dishonour your glorious throne."*
> *(Jeremiah 14:20-21)*

His message, however, like that of Isaiah, was not all doom and gloom. He, too, spoke of a future in which God would make a new covenant with His people; one written not on tablets of stone, but on the hearts of individuals.

> *"This is the covenant that I will make with the people of Israel,*
> *after that time' declares the Lord.*
> *'I will put my law in their minds*
> *and write it on their hearts.*
> *I will be their God,*
> *and they will be my people."*
> *(Jeremiah 31:33)*

In this same chapter, Chapter 31, God also declares:

> *"This is what the L*ORD *says,*
> *he who appoints the sun*
> *to shine by day,*
> *who decrees the moon and stars*
> *to shine by night,*
> *who stirs up the sea so that its waves roar –*
> *The L*ORD *Almighty is his name:*
> *'Only if those decrees vanish from my sight,'*
> *declares the L*ORD,
> *'will Israel ever cease*
> *being a nation before me."*
> *(Jeremiah 31:37)*

The fulfilment of this promise was evident in 1948 when Israel was given back her land and declared a nation.

Lamentations.

The full horror of seeing his nation going into exile, after having been utterly crushed by the Babylonians, is expressed by Jeremiah in his book Lamentations. This book takes the form of five laments, written as five poems, each from a different point of view.

The first lament is that of the city of Jerusalem, referred to as "she".

What Jeremiah found to be especially painful was that it was God's city that had been reduced to ruins; His holy Temple was no more.

> *"The enemy laid hands*
> *on all her treasures;*
> *she saw pagan nations*
> *enter her sanctuary –*
> *those you had forbidden*
> *to enter your assembly."*
> *(Lamentations 1:10)*

The second lament focuses on God. He has caused all this devastation and suffering as a punishment for the continual unconfessed sins of His people.

> *"The LORD has done what he planned;*
> *He has fulfilled his word,*
> *which he decreed long ago.*
> *He has overthrown you without pity,*
> *he has let the enemy gloat over you,*
> *he has exalted the horn of your foes."*
> *(Lamentations 2:17)*

Lamentations

The third lament is a very personal one. In it Jeremiah expresses his own sufferings.

> *"He pierced my heart*
> *with arrows from his quiver.*
> *I became the laughing-stock of all my people;*
> *they mock me in song all day long.*
> *He has filled me with bitter herbs*
> *and given me gall to drink.".*
> *(Lamentations 3:13-15)*

But Jeremiah also reflects on the fact that in His mercy God did not wipe out the whole nation; in sending them into exile, there was an opportunity for them to be rebuild into a nation once again.

> *"Because of the LORD'S great love we are not consumed.*
> *for his compassions never fail.*
> *They are new every morning;*
> *great is your faithfulness."*
> *(Lamentations 3:22-23)*

In the fourth lament, Jeremiah is concerned with the people of his nation and the consequences of their sin. However, there will be an end to the punishment for their God is a God of deliverance.

> *"Your punishment will end Daughter of Zion;*
> *He will not prolong your exile.*
> *But he will punish your sin, Daughter Edom*
> *and expose your wickedness."*
> *(Lamentations 4:22)*

The last lament is a prayer, pleading with God to show His mercy as the exile is causing so much suffering.

Lamentations

*"Restore us to yourself, L*ORD*, that we may return;*
renew our days as of old
unless you have utterly rejected us
and are angry with us beyond measure."
(Lamentations 5:21-22)

Ezekiel

The book of Ezekiel is one of the least popular books of the Bible because in it Ezekiel speaks of the severity of God's judgement with little encouragement. He was born into a priestly family in Judah not long before the Babylonians appeared on the scene. Indeed he was just 25 years old when he was deported to Babylon along with the cream of Jewish society. At the age of 30 when he was due to commence his priestly duties, had he been in Jerusalem, God called him to be a prophet. God referred to him as, 'son of man', a title not used for any other Old Testament prophet but taken up by Jesus in the New Testament.

'He said: *"Son of man, I am sending you to the Israelites, to a rebellious nation that has rebelled against me; they and their ancestors have been in revolt against me to this very day.*
The people to whom I am sending you are obstinate and stubborn …… they will know that a prophet has been among them. …..And you, son of man, do not be afraid of them or their words." (Ezekiel 2:3 4b & 6b).

Much of Ezekiel's message was more visual than verbal and very symbolic. The opening paragraphs of the first chapter have a description of a vision that Ezekiel saw. It is a very weird combination of human, animal and angel which possibly symbolises all of God's living creation. Above this apparition, he sees Creator God seated on His throne.

"This was the appearance of the likeness of the glory of the Lord." (Ezekiel 1:28b).

The lower part of the vision was of four wheels.

"This was the appearance and structure of the wheels: they sparkled like topaz, and all four looked alike. Each

Ezekiel

appeared to be made like a wheel intersecting a wheel. As they moved, they would go in any one of the four directions the creatures faced; the wheels did not change direction as the creatures went. Their rims were high and awesome, and all four rims were full of eyes all around." (Ezekiel 1:16-18).

This symbolises the mobility of God; He can be anywhere and everywhere. This vision was so important to Ezekiel and his fellow countrymen in Babylon, for up to this point, they had believed that their God was static over Jerusalem. It was comforting to know that their God was with them in Babylon. The eyes on the rims of the wheels give us to understand that God can see everything everywhere. God then gave Ezekiel a scroll on which to write the prophecies that he was to deliver; these were words of lamentation and curses. He was then told to eat the scroll which was sweet in his mouth.

Many prophets had warned the people that their wickedness would lead to exile and Jeremiah had said that Jerusalem would be gutted. However there were three deportations to Babylon and the Babylonians had conquered the city, but it remained a city. The quick response of the people was that Jeremiah had exaggerated the extent of their punishment by God. Ezekiel had to teach them that God always keeps His word; they were to suffer not only exile for at least the life span of a generation but also the loss of their beloved city and its temple.

This message was demonstrated to them by a completely silent Ezekiel in six different ways. Firstly he drew it on a slab of clay – the city being attacked with battering rams. He then had to lie on his left side for 390 days and on his right side for another 40 days to symbolise how long the house of Israel had been disobeying God and then the house of Judah (390 years and 40 years).

Ezekiel

Ezekiel also had to go on a diet of bread and water for a protracted period to symbolise the shortage of food during the siege of Jerusalem. God asked him to cook his bread over a fire fuelled by his own excrement. This was a step too far for the prophet and when he protested a merciful God allowed him to use cow dung. He had to shave his head and beard with a sword and divide the hair into three piles.

The first pile was to be burnt at the end of the siege of Jerusalem. The second pile was to be scattered around the model city with the sword and the third pile was to be thrown into the air and thus scattered abroad which was the fate of those still alive. He then had to put on his clothes in a bag, dig a hole in a wall and creep out through the wall at night. This was to explain what would happen to King Zedekiah when Jerusalem fell. The hardest demand God made on him was to suffer the death of his wife without mourning. When Jerusalem finally fell, the people were so stunned that they refused to believe it and would not even cry.

God wanted to use the time of exile not just to punish His people, but to reform them too. Ezekiel had to impress upon the exiles that the three major reasons for God's judgement upon them was their idolatry, immorality and ingratitude. To do this, Ezekiel used parables through which he made them understand that their true state before God was worse than they realised. They had to learn that each individual is responsible for their personal state; they could not blame their ancestors.

"The one who sins is the one who will die. The child will not share the guilt of the parent, nor will the parent share the guilt of the child. The righteousness of the righteous will be credited to him, and the wickedness of the wicked will be charged against them." (Ezekiel 18:20).

Ezekiel

They were also taught that past sins can be forgiven and that what mattered was the state of their soul at the time of death. Conversely if they had led a blameless life in their youth but had fallen into sinful ways in later life, which were unrepented, it was this state that would be judged.

"Therefore, you Israelites, I will judge each of you according to your own ways, declares the Sovereign LORD. Repent! Turn away from all your offences; then sin will not be your downfall. Rid yourselves of all the offences you have committed, and get a new heart and a new spirit. Why will you die, people of Israel? For I take no pleasure in the death of anyone, declares the Sovereign LORD. Repent and live!" (Ezekiel 18:30-32).

The middle chapters of this book tell of God's judgement on the surrounding nations of Israel. These nations exalted in her downfall and did nothing to help her when she was attacked. God will pay back in full, those who exploit the fall of His people.

The last seven chapters were written after the fall of Jerusalem and are far more optimistic, for he predicts the people's return from exile. Even though Ezekiel was in Babylon and a very long way from Jerusalem, God saw him as a watchman there, posted to warn the people of coming disaster. This was a heavy responsibility which if not carried out, meant he would answer before God for their ignorance.

"When I say to the wicked, "You wicked person, you will surely die," and you do not speak out to dissuade them from their ways, that wicked person will die for their sin, and I will hold you accountable for their blood. But if you do warn the wicked person to turn from their ways and they do not do so, they will die for their sin, though you yourself will be saved. (Ezekiel 33:8-9).

Ezekiel

This applied to all the spiritual shepherds of God's people, all the leaders who had neglected their duties.

'You have not strengthened the weak or healed those who are ill or bound up the injured. You have not brought back the strays or searched for the lost. You have ruled them harshly and brutally'. (Ezekiel 34:4).

This is what the Sovereign LORD says: 'I am against the shepherds and will hold them accountable for my flock. I will remove them from tending the flock so that the shepherds can no longer feed themselves. I will rescue my flock from their mouths, and it will no longer be food for them. (Ezekiel 34:10).

God's promise to His people was that He would rescue them and return them to their land where they would be greatly blessed.

'The trees will yield their fruit and the ground will yield its crops; the people will be secure in their land. They will know that I am the LORD, when I break the bars of their yoke and rescue them from the hands of those who enslaved them' '(Ezekiel 34:27).

Another promise that He made to them was demonstrated by Ezekiel holding up two sticks on which he wrote Judah and Ephraim. These he was instructed to hold together in his hand so that they became one stick. God was saying that He was causing His people to become one kingdom again. However by far the best promise was that the Temple would be rebuilt. Ezekiel is given the detailed measurements for a temple, far larger than Solomon's Temple, but it has no 'holy of holies', no ark of the covenant and no table of the showbread. It was a temple in which the glory of God returns.

Ezekiel

Such a temple has yet to be seen in Jerusalem! The returning exiles built a very small one and King Herod improved upon this building to make it grander, but still not according to Ezekiel's plans.

In the final chapter Ezekiel has a vision of a new river flowing from beneath the Temple as it goes down to the Dead Sea it becomes deeper and deeper. When it enters the Dead Sea it brings life there so that fish live in it. There is also a vision of the city gates being re-erected to allow the city to once again have peace and prosperity. God always gives hope to His people, there must be judgement and punishment because He is a holy God, but He will always restore His people. His vengeance is for those who mistreat His people.

Daniel

Daniel, like Ezekiel, was an exile to Babylon whilst still a very young man. He was chosen, along with three of his friends, (Shadrach, Meshach and Abednego) to be trained for service in the king's palace. The four of them were given Babylonian names and put on a very rich diet to be fattened up. This did not please them as they desired to keep God's dietary laws and requested a diet of vegetables and water.

They found favour with the official who agreed to do it for ten days and see the result. As they looked healthier and better nourished than the other young men they were allowed to continue. They realised that God had given them the courage to make a stand on this small matter and were ready for the greater challenges when they came along. At the end of the training period they were brought before the king who questioned them.

"In every matter of wisdom and understanding about which the king questioned them, he found them ten times better than all the magicians and enchanters in his whole kingdom." (Daniel 1:20).

Indeed when the king requested his magicians to tell him his dream and its interpretation, they all failed to do so. The king was so angry that he called for the execution of all the wise men in Babylon, including Daniel and his friends. When Daniel was told the reason for such a harsh edict, he requested an audience with the king, and promised that he would bring an interpretation, given time. Then he asked his friends to pray for God's mercy to reveal this mystery. The boldness of their faith that God knew the answer the king was seeking was justified.

During the night in a vision all was revealed to Daniel.

Daniel

He immediately praised his God.

> *"Praise be the name of God for ever and ever;*
> *wisdom and power are His*
> *He changes times and seasons;*
> *he deposes kings and raises up others.*
> *He gives wisdom to the wise*
> *and knowledge to the discerning.*
> *He reveals deep and hidden things;*
> *he knows what lies in darkness,*
> *and light dwells within Him.*
> *I thank and praise you, God of my ancestors;*
> *you have given me wisdom and power,*
> *you have made known to me what we asked of you,*
> *you have made known to us the dream of the King."*
> *(Daniel 2:20-23)*

As he now had the interpretation he asked the official not to go ahead with the executions, but to take him to the king. He explained to the king that the dream was from his God, who had given him the meaning of it.

The dream was of a large statue made of different metals from head to foot. Each part of the statue represented different empires; the golden head was the Babylonian King. After his empire would come one of inferior metal which in turn would be succeeded by two more of inferior materials; the last would be a mixture of iron and clay that would not remain together. At this time God would set up an indestructible kingdom which would crush all kingdoms but would itself endure forever.

Why the dream? It was to warn the king that his God was in charge of all that happened to all earthly kingdoms. It was He who caused the rise and fall of kingdoms. Despite the warning the king set up a golden statue of himself and demanded that all his subjects should bow down to it. The three friends of Daniel openly refused to do so. Their punishment for such disobedience was to be thrown into a fiery furnace. The king did give them a chance to rescind their decision when the punishment was put to them, but even facing the fiery furnace, they were adamant.

"If we are thrown into the blazing furnace, the God we serve is able to save us from it, and he will deliver us from 'Your Majesty's' hand." (Daniel 3:17).

Such boldness caused the king to have the furnace heated seven times hotter than usual. However, their God delights in their faith in Him; such faith and love are always rewarded. The three men were tightly bound before being thrown into the furnace, but God joined them in it, releasing them from their bounds and keeping them free from any effects of the fire. The king saw that there were four figures in the furnace and that all were moving freely. He demanded for the furnace to be opened and called the men to come out.

"They saw that the fire had not harmed their bodies, nor was a hair on their heads singed; their robes were not scorched, and there was no smell of fire on them."(Daniel 3:27).

This had a profound effect upon the king, who immediately praised their God for what He had done for them, and made a decree that none of his subjects should speak a word against their God. He also gave the three Israelites positions of authority. Nevertheless, he was still a king who was immensely proud of his own achievements.

"Is not this great Babylon I have built as the royal residence, by my mighty power and for the glory of my

majesty?" (Daniel 4:30).

God had warned him through another dream, interpreted by Daniel, that he was to acknowledge the Most High God who had given to him his kingdom and all his prosperity, and that if he refused to do so, his punishment would be for him to lose his sanity and be driven away from people to live with the wild animals until such time as he humbled himself before God.

Seven years later, he lifted his eyes to heaven and declared that God was indeed the God of all the earth; that His dominion was an eternal dominion. God restored him to his throne and made him greater than before.

His successor King Belshazzar did not have time for the God of the Jews, or indeed for the vessels stolen from the temple. He used these in an orgy; during which he saw a finger write words on the wall. Daniel was called to interpret. Daniel explained that the words meant; 'your reign is over, you do not measure up and your kingdom is divided.' That night the Persians attacked Babylon and the king was killed.

When a very old man, Daniel had his faith in God severely tried. At this time Daniel was serving in the empire of the Medes and the Persians (under King Darius) who had taken over Babylon.

The king made an edict that for thirty days no one should worship any god, but the king. Daniel refused to stop praying to his God, and he made certain that all should know this, for he prayed with his windows wide open. The penalty for such disobedience was to be thrown into the lions' den.

When the king was told of Daniel's praying, he was sorry to have to carry out the punishment for he greatly valued Daniel's wisdom, but he could not go against his word. Daniel

Daniel

was ordered to be thrown to the lions but the king said to him,

"May your God, whom you serve continually rescue you!" (Daniel 6:16).

That prayer and Daniel's faith proved the power of God to keep His loyal servant. An angel closed the mouth of the lions so that when the king returned in the morning and called to Daniel he replied that all was well with him.

Daniel answered, 'May the king live for ever! My God sent his angel, and he shut the mouths of the lions. They have not hurt me, because I was found innocent in his sight. Nor have I ever done any wrong before you, Your Majesty.' (Daniel 6:22).

Such bold faith caused the king to convert to the God of the Jews. As a result the king wrote a decree that all his subjects were to worship Daniel's God.

*"For He is the living God
and He endures for ever;
his kingdom will not be destroyed,
his dominion will never end.
He rescues and He saves;
he performs signs and wonders
in the heavens and on the earth.
He has rescued Daniel
from the power of the lions."
(Daniel 6:26-27)*

The last six chapters of the book of Daniel tell of his visions from God. They were written in Hebrew, so were intended for his own people, whereas the earlier chapters had been written in Aramaic, the universal language of the day.

Daniel

These prophetic visions cover two periods of time, one leading up to the first coming of the Messiah and one leading up to the second. But the predictions he makes are so detailed and have proved to be so accurate in regards to those already fulfilled that we cannot doubt that God is in charge.

That is not to deny our free will, even though He steers the course of events. Daniel fuses together the two comings of the Messiah with no detail of the period of time between the two events. This makes the understanding of these chapters very difficult.

What was God's purpose in giving Daniel these visions? There would be a period of 400 years between the end of the prophetical period and the coming of John the Baptist who issued in the New Testament period.

These prophetical visions of Daniel would give God's people encouragement that He was going to send His Messiah to them.

In these last chapters they are encouraged to do a number of things as they lay hold of the future: to stand firm, to do exploits, to endure suffering, to resist evil and to find rest.

God was preparing them to trust Him through all their trials because He knows the end from the beginning. They are also a warning to all unbelievers who want to be empire builders that God's Son will ultimately replace them all.

Hosea

Hosea was the last prophet to speak to the people of the northern kingdom before they were conquered and sent into exile. It is God's final appeal to the ten tribes before they disappear. It is therefore a book full of God's emotion. He had made a covenant of love with them, but despite the many warnings from the prophets, they had chosen to go their own way and had given little thought to the keeping of God's law.

To express how deeply God felt about their betrayal of the covenant, Hosea was told to marry a prostitute and to have children with her.

The names of the children carried a message to the nation. The eldest, a boy, was called Jezreel, which means, 'God sows it'. He was a rebellious child who needed much discipline. The next child, a girl, was called Lo-Ruhamah, meaning 'not pitied' – a child deprived of her mother's love. The third child, a boy, called Lo-Amric, meaning 'not my people' was fathered by someone else, not Hosea, and so the boy was disowned.

The children's names express how God was dealing with His people. He had disciplined them, had tried depriving them of His love and favour, but nothing caused them to return to Him and so He was about to disown them.

Once the children were born, his wife returned to her old occupation. Hosea sought her out, brought her home and for a while disciplined her, before receiving her again as his wife.

'For the Israelites will live for many days without king or prince, without sacrifice or sacred stones, without ephod or household gods. Afterwards the Israelites will return and seek the LORD *their God and David their king. They will come*

trembling to the L<small>ORD</small> *and to his blessings in the last days.'*
(Hosea 3:4-5)

As with all the previous prophets, Hosea enumerates the nation's sins but especially their continual unfaithfulness toward God in contrast to His faithful, loving kindness to them.

> *"What can I do with you, Ephraim?*
> *What can I do with you, Judah?*
> *Your love is like the morning mist,*
> *like the early dew that disappears.*
> *Therefore I cut you in pieces with my prophets,*
> *I killed you with the words of my mouth;*
> *then my judgments go forth like the sun.*
> *For I desire mercy, not sacrifice,*
> *and acknowledgement of God rather than burnt offerings."*
> *(Hosea 6:4-6)*

God has longed for their repentance, but it must be a lasting change of heart. Their indifference to Him has to be punished for He is a just God. He cannot let them off even though He finds it so hard to let them go.

> *"Return, Israel, to the* L<small>ORD</small> *your God.*
> *Yours sins have been your downfall!*
> *Take words with you and return to the Lord.*
> *Say to Him: 'Forgive all our sins*
> *and receive us graciously*
> *that we may offer the fruit of our lips."*
> *(Hosea 14:1-2)*

> *"I will heal their waywardness*
> *and love them freely,*
> *For my anger has turned away from them.*
> *I will be like the dew to Israel;*

he will blossom like a lily.
Like a cedar of Lebanon
he will send down his roots."
(Hosea 14:4-5)

Father God has opened His heart to them, declared His great love for them but they have the final choice, to continue sinning, will mean banishment from God's protection.

"Who is wise? Let them realise these things.
Who is discerning? Let them understand.
The ways of the LORD are right;
the righteous walk in them,
but the rebellious stumble in them."
(Hosea 14:9)

Joel

The book of Joel was written when the nation had suffered a dreadful plague of locusts. Such a plague was very unusual in Israel, and so Joel told the people that he saw God's hand in it. It was a warning from God that if they continued living in their sinful ways, then something even worse would happen. As it was this disaster had caused all public worship to cease. The vineyards, orchards and olive groves had been destroyed.

The nation faced drought, bush fires and starvation. It was indeed a serious warning; a reminder of the judgement of God. Joel exhorts the priests and all the elders to call the people to repentance.

> "Blow the trumpet in Zion
> sound the alarm on my holy hill
> Let all who live in the land tremble,
> for the day of the LORD is coming.
> It is close at hand."
> (Joel 2:1)

Joel warns that if they fail to heed this warning, they will lose their land altogether; they will be conquered by a stronger nation.

> "Even now,' declares the Lord,
> 'return to me with all your heart,
> with fasting and weeping and mourning.'
> Rend your heart and not your garments.
> Return to the Lord your God,
> for he is gracious and compassionate,
> slow to anger and abounding in love,
> and he relents from sending calamity."
> (Joel 2:12-13)

Joel

Unfortunately the reaction of the people was one of fear rather than true repentance, even though they were shown how good and generous the Lord was to the after the locusts had moved on. Again Joel exhorts them,

> "Surely he has done great things!
> Do not be afraid, land of Judah;
> be glad and rejoice.
> Surely the LORD has done great things
> Do not be afraid, you wild animals,
> for the pastures in the wilderness are becoming green.
> The trees are bearing their fruit;
> the fig-tree and the vine yield their riches.
> Be glad, people of Zion, rejoice in the Lord your God." (Joel 2: 20b-23b)

> "I will repay you for the years the locusts have eaten…..-
> "Then you will know that I am in Israel,
> that I am the LORD your God,
> and that there is no other;
> never again will my people be shamed."
> (Joel 2:25b; 27)

At this time in the history of God's people, only the priests and prophets received God's Spirit to impart His ways and guidance to the people and they were judged as a nation. However, Joel, like Ezekiel, looked forward to a time when everyone, every single individual who belonged to God would have His Spirit.

> "And afterwards,
> I will pour out my Spirit on all people.
> Your sons and daughters will prophesy,
> your old men will dream dreams,

> *your young men will see visions.*
> *Even on my servants, both men and women,*
> *I will pour out my Spirit in those days."*
> *(Joel 2:28-29)*

Salvation was to be the right of the individual who called upon, and had faith in His name.

Joel completes his message by prophesying of a time to come when God would call all nations to meet with Him that He might judge them. The criteria by which they will be judged is how they have treated God's people.

> *"Multitudes, multitudes in the valley of decision!*
> *For the day of the LORD is near in the valley of decision."*
> *The sun and moon will be darkened, and the stars no longer shine. The LORD will roar from Zion*
> *and thunder from Jerusalem."*
> *(Joel 3:14-16)*

The promise for His people, at that time, is that He will be their stronghold and that never again would foreigners invade Jerusalem.

Amos

Amos was not trained to be either a prophet or priest but a poor farmer in a small town in the southern kingdom of Judah whom the Lord spoke to through dreams and visions. It was a surprise to him to be called of God to go to the northern kingdom of Israel to warn the people that God was about to punish them for their sinful ways unless they repented and came back to God.

God gave him two visions concerning the northern kingdom, one of a plague of locusts who stripped the land clean. When Amos saw this, his reaction was,

> "Sovereign LORD, forgive! How can Jacob survive? He is so small! " (Amos 7:2)

The second vision was of a fire which devoured the land. Again Amos protested against such a punishment and again the Lord relented. .

The fervent prayers of Amos were powerful enough to cause God to change His mind, but not His character.

When Amos was first sent to Israel his message that the Lord gave him was of the curses that God was going to bring on all the neighbouring nations including Judah for all their sinful ways which a just God could not ignore.

It was a warning to them to change their way The people of Israel soon came to listen, for they loved to hear of God's anger with their neighbours. However, it was a different matter when Amos began to speak of God's thoughts concerning their lifestyle. He spoke of the relationship that the Lord had with their ancestors and all that He had done for them and yet they had turned their backs on Him. Nevertheless He, the

Amos

Lord, was merciful and would not punish without warning.

> *"Surely the Sovereign LORD does nothing*
> *without revealing his plan*
> *to his servants the prophets."*
> *(Amos 3:7)*

If the warning is not heeded then God would allow the enemy to overrun the land, but always a faithful remnant will be saved.

Amos warned that every part of society was corrupt; even their religious feasts which were all show, had no bearing upon their way of living. Though Israel's utter contempt of the warnings from Amos lead to their downfall by Assyria, yet as with his fellow prophet Amos' final words to them was a message of hope:

> *"In that day I will restore*
> *David's fallen shelter -.*
> *I will repair its broken walls,*
> *and restore its ruins*
> *and will rebuild it as it used to be,*
> *so that they may possess the remnant of Edom*
> *and all the nations that bear my name."*
> *(Amos 9:11-12)*

Obadiah

The book of Obadiah, the shortest in the Old Testament, tells of his vision from the Lord for the country of Edom. Edom was situated south east of the Jordan. The people of Edom traced their ancestry back to Esau, the brother of Jacob / Israel, and so were related to God's people, the Israelites. However they showed nothing but hatred toward them, and greatly delighted in seeing them defeated.

Obadiah's vision came very soon after the southern kingdom of Judah was taken into exile by the Babylonians. It was a warning to the Edomite's that God would punish them for their pride in their invincibility. They felt that because they were a mountainous people, no nation could capture their main cities, high on Mount Seir.

> *"In that day", 'declares the Lord',*
> *"Will I not destroy the wise men of Edom,*
> *those of understanding in the mountains of Esau?*
> *Your warriors, O Teman, will be terrified,*
> *and everyone in Esau's mountains*
> *Will be cut down in the slaughter.*
> *Because of the violence against your brother Jacob,*
> *you will be covered with shame;*
> *You will be destroyed for ever."*
> *(Obadiah: 8-10)*

The God of the Israelites whom they had despised and belittled, they were to find out was in fact the God of all creation who would bring justice and vengeance to all nations who treated His people badly. This is the message of Obadiah in the last few verses of his book.

> *"The day of the LORD is near for all nations.*
> *As you have done, it will be done to you;*

Obadiah

your deeds will return upon your own head."
(Obadiah: 15)

"Deliverers will go up on Mount Zion
to govern the mountain of Esau
and the kingdom will be the LORD'S "
(Obadiah: 21)

Jonah

The book of Jonah gives us a very clear understanding of God's great compassion and mercy towards all His creation. In the opening chapter God asks His prophet Jonah who lived in Israel, to go to Nineveh, the capital of Assyria with a warning. He was to tell them,

"Forty more days and Nineveh will be overturned."
(Jonah 3:1)

This warning was to be given because God had seen their wickedness. However Jonah had had much experience of the ways of His God and knew that if this warning was taken seriously then God would accept their repentance and withhold the punishment. Jonah felt that if a punishment was due, it should be given there and then; God's name would not be glorified if He were too soft with the nations. As a result Jonah ran away, taking a ship going in the opposite direction.

God caused a violent storm which Jonah knew was his fault and so he agreed for the sailors to throw him overboard. His dead body was swallowed by a whale which vomited him on dry land. Here God brought him back to life again. Jonah's life was restored for him to do the work which God had asked him to do.

Jonah went to Nineveh and for three days he walked through the city proclaiming the message God had given him. "The Ninevites believed God. They declared a fast, and all of them, from the greatest to the least, put on sackcloth." (Jonah 3:5). The king of Assyria when he heard the news, also greatly humbled himself and proclaimed,

"Let everyone call urgently on God. Let them give up their evil ways and their violence. Who knows? God may yet relent and with compassion turn from His fierce anger so that we

will not perish." (Jonah 3:8b-9)

God was moved by their sincere repentance and did withhold His hand from allowing the destruction He had threatened. This did not please Jonah, who did not rejoice in the wonderful effect his words had. On the contrary he felt very vexed with God for changing His mind, and told Him so.

*"I knew that you are a gracious and compassionate God, slow to anger and abounding in love, a God who relents from sending calamity. Now, L*ORD *take away my life, for it is better for me to die than to live." (Jonah 4:2-3)*

God rebuked him for sulking but provided a plant to shade him as he sat in the fierce heat of the sun. Overnight the plant shrivelled and died and this too made Jonah angry. Again God rebuked him for being more concerned about the plant dying than he was about the 120 thousand innocent children in Nineveh who would have died had the city been destroyed.

Micah

The prophet Micah lived at the same time as the prophet Isaiah. Isaiah was born in the king's palace for he was a cousin of the king in Jerusalem and his message was for the king and the leaders of the land, whereas Micah was born in a country village also in Judah, but his passion was for the people living around him; the poor who were exploited by the rich.

In his first vision Micah saw that the wickedness of the capital cities, Samaria in the north and Jerusalem in the south, had spread to the countryside and that the people in the villages around him were practicing the idolatry and immorality for which the cities had been condemned. His sensitive spirit was broken when he realised that a just God must punish these people who were close to him too, if they were to continue in their sin.

> *"Because of this I will weep and wail;*
> *I will go about barefoot and naked.*
> *I will howl like a jackal*
> *and moan like an owl.*
> *For Samaria's plague is incurable;*
> *it has spread to Judah.*
> *It has reached the very gate of my people,*
> *even to Jerusalem itself."*
> *(Micah 1:8-9)*

His message in these opening chapters is one of crime and punishment, but to make it more personal and vivid to these countryside people, he takes the names of the villages and incorporates them into his message.

However like his fellow prophets, he points out that the present corrupt state and the impending punishment is not the end of the story. In the middle section of his book he brings the good news. God is going to send a king of the line of David who will

Micah

bring salvation to His people. Micah even gives us information about the town in which He would be born, 700 years before He arrived!

> "But you, Bethlehem Ephrathah,
> though you are small among the clans of Judah,
> out of you will come for me
> one who will be ruler over Israel,
> Whose origins are from of old,
> from ancient times."
> (Micah 5:2)

Micah also has prophecy concerning the second coming of Jesus which has yet to be fulfilled. When Jesus comes again, He will set up His kingdom on earth and His headquarters will be in Jerusalem.

> "Many nations will come and say,
>
> "Come, let us go up to the mountain of the LORD,
> to the temple of the God of Jacob.
> He will teach us his ways,
> so that we may walk in his paths.'
> The law will go out from Zion,
> the word of the LORD from Jerusalem.
> He will judge between many peoples
> And will settle disputes for strong nations far and wide."
> (Micah 4:2-3)

In the final two chapters of the book, we see God as the counsel for prosecution and Micah as the counsel for defence. The people of Judah are in the dock. God reminds them of all He has done for them in past years and how they have gone their own way, regardless of His warnings.,

> "He has showed you, O mortal, what is good.

Micah

And what does the L<small>ORD</small> require of you?
To act justly and to love mercy
And to walk humble with your God."
(Micah 6:8)

Micah is so very unhappy in this court scene as he hears the just punishment meted out to Israel, but his mercy turns to rejoicing when he realises that the God of Justice is also the God of mercy.

"Who is a God like you,
Who pardons sin and forgives the transgression
of the remnant of his inheritance?
You do not stay angry for ever,
but delight to show mercy."
(Micah 7:18)

Nahum

Both Jonah and Nahum were sent from Israel to Nineveh, the capital of Assyria with a word from God.

Jonah's was a warning of which they took heed, but Nahum's, given 150 years later, was a proclamation. Jonah spoke of God's anger at the way they were living and their cruelty towards those they had conquered. His word was met with a positive response and their repentance lasted for a time but they did lapse into their former ways.

When Nahum came on the scene, Assyria was the major world power. They were so very proud of their achievements and so very cruel to those they had conquered which included the northern state, Israel. This time God's righteous anger had reached boiling point, no more warnings. Nahum's message was one of disaster for God's enemies, but also one of deliverance for His friends.

> *"Who can withstand his indignation?*
> *Who can endure his fierce anger?*
> *His wrath is poured out like fire;*
> *the rocks are shattered before him.*
> *The LORD is good,*
> *a refuge in times of trouble.*
> *He cares for those who trust in him,*
> *but with an overwhelming flood*
> *he will make an end of Nineveh;*
> *he will pursue his foes into the realm of darkness."*
> *(Nahum 1:6-8)*

Nahum gives a very detailed account of how Nineveh would be attacked by an army in red uniforms who completely sacked the city, stripping it of all its wealth and causing the inhabitants to flee. In fact when the Babylonians attacked Assyria they were dressed in scarlet uniforms!

This was to be the end of Assyria; she was destroyed forever! Nineveh was lost for centuries, covered by a desert.

> *"Nothing can heal you;*
> *Your wound is fatal.*
> *All who hear the news about you*
> *clap their hands at your fall*
> *for who has not felt your endless cruelty?"*
> *(Nahum 3:19)*

It was God who allowed Assyria to become a mighty empire but when they showed pride in their achievements and had such disdain for all other nations, including God's people, then God orchestrated their defeat.

Habakkuk

Habakkuk was writing during a time of great turmoil for his nation, the kingdom of Judah. Assyria had been conquered by the Babylonians who were busy expanding their empire in the countries surrounding Judah, but had not as yet approached his nation.

Whereas in most of the prophetic books, the prophecy was given by God to the prophet who then spoke it out to the peoples to whom it was intended, Habakkuk begins his book by addressing God with a series of questions which he required to be answered. It is a prayer of complaint because he felt that God could do more for His people; why were the wicked not suffering more? God's answer was that the Babylonians were coming to punish the wicked. This was not the answer Habakkuk wanted to hear!

Why would God use a wicked nation to punish the wicked in his land; it would mean the innocent would suffer too. God answered that there would be a means of escape for the good.

> *"You, my Rock, have ordained them (Babylonians) to punish. (Judah)*
> *Your eyes are too pure to look on evil;*
> *you cannot tolerate wrongdoing.*
> *Why then do you tolerate the treacherous?*
> *Why are you silent while the wicked*
> *swallow up those more righteous than themselves?"*
> *(Habakkuk 1:12b-13)*

When God was about to answer this complaint, He told Habakkuk to write down what He was about to tell him on a tablet so that the answer would be spread amongst His people.

Habakkuk

> *"For the revelation awaits an appointed time;*
> *it speaks of the end*
> *and will not prove false.*
> *Though it linger, wait for it;*
> *it will certainly come*
> *and will not delay.*
> *See, the enemy is puffed up;*
> *his desires are not upright –*
> *but the righteous will live by his faith."*
> (Habakkuk 2:3-4)

God's promise is that those who remain faithful to Him throughout all the troubles which were to come upon their nation, would be saved because of their faithfulness. If they remained true to God throughout all the impending disasters then He would remain true to them and bring them through.

God also promised Habakkuk that though Babylon would be the instrument He would use to punish the wicked in Judah, He knew of the great wickedness of Babylon itself and would bring that mighty nation crashing down, to rise no more. Habakkuk was to speak out five woes or curses against Babylon, listing the many evils of which they were guilty. All of these evils were against humanity not God for they were not God's people and could not be expected to keep God's laws.

> *"Because you have plundered many nations*
> *the peoples who are left will plunder you.*
> *For you have shed man's blood;*
> *You have destroyed lands and cities and*
> *everyone in them."*
> (Habakkuk 2:8)

Once He had given Habakkuk his answer, God declared that He was in His holy temple and He did not want any more questions!

Habakkuk

As Habakkuk meditated on all that God had said he realised that God had a far larger view of things than he did and could see into the future. This realisation caused his whole attitude toward God to change. The final chapter of his book is a song of praise in which he reflects on God's majesty and power in creation; his only plea is that God's wrath would be tempered with mercy.

> *"I stand in awe of your deeds, LORD.*
> *Repeat them in our day,*
> *In our time make them known;*
> *in wrath remember mercy."*
> *(Habakkuk 3:2)*

Habakkuk knows that he can be counted amongst the faithful and so though he trembles at the thought of what God is going to do, he has hope that all will be well in the end

> *"Though the fig tree does not bud*
> *and there are no grapes on the vines,*
> *though the olive crop fails*
> *and the fields produce no food,*
> *though there are no sheep in the pen*
> *and no cattle in the stalls,*
> *yet I will rejoice in the Lord,*
> *I will be joyful in God my Saviour.*
> *The Sovereign LORD is my strength;*
> *he makes my feet like the feet of a deer,*
> *he enables me to go on the heights."*
> *(Habakkuk 3:17-19)*

Zephaniah

Zephaniah is yet another prophet who brings a stark message of warning to God's people. He is speaking on behalf of a God who is eager to show His mercy on a nation He loves, and so in His long suffering He sends prophet after prophet with much the same message of warning that a holy God cannot allow wrong doing to go unpunished but always there is a way out if the people repent and seek His mercy; He is eager to forgive. They must come back to Him and live holy lives.

Zephaniah begins his message by reminding the people of Judah that their God is a God of the whole world and that the time will come when He will wipe out all creation because of its wickedness. However before that time He is warning Judah that He will not tolerate their practice of worshiping other gods.

> *"and neither seek the LORD not enquire of Him*
> *Be silent before the Sovereign LORD, For the day of the LORD is near."*
> *(Zephaniah 1:6-7)*

"The day of the Lord", Zephaniah warns is a time of great disaster, causing wailing and death to those who have been most defiant against God's laws.

When judgement comes, everyone will know; their whole world will be turned upside down. Such a warning is as always, tempered by His mercy.

> *"Seek the LORD all you humble of the land,*
> *you who do what he commands.*
> *Seek righteousness, seek humility;*
> *perhaps you will be sheltered*

Zephaniah

> *on the day of the Lord's anger."*
> *(Zephaniah 2:3)*

Zephaniah also has a message for all the nations who surround Judah and for those further afield like Assyria. They too will be judged for their attitude towards God's people.

> *"This is what they will get in return for their pride,*
> *for insulting and mocking*
> *the people of the LORD Almighty*
> *The LORD will be awesome to them*
> *When He destroys all the gods of the earth.*
> *Distant nations will bow down to him,*
> *all of them in their own lands"*
> *(Zephaniah 2:10-11)*

This is a prophecy yet to be fulfilled as it looks forward to the second coming of Jesus and His reign on earth.

Zephaniah also looks forward to the time when Israel will be one people under the reign of Jesus.

> *"The LORD, the King of Israel, is with you;*
> *never again will you fear any harm.*
> *On that day they will say to Jerusalem, 'Do not fear, Zion;*
> *do not let your hands hang limp.*
> *The LORD your God is with you,*
> *The Mighty Warrior who saves.*
> *He will take great delight in you;*
> *In his love he will no longer rebuke you;*
> *but will rejoice over you with singing."*
> *(Zephaniah 3:15b-17)*

Haggai

These three books, the last books in the Old Testament were written after the Israelites returned from exile. Their return was sanctioned by King Cyrus of Persia who commissioned the returning exiles to build a temple in which to pray to their God for Him. Only about 50,000 Jews returned on this occasion for most were successful business men and did not want to travel to a land they did not know where prospects were bleak.

Those who did make the journey back to Jerusalem did begin to lay the foundations for a new temple using a subsidy that Cyrus had given them. However when Cyrus was replaced on the throne by Darius the subsidy ceased.

The enthusiasm for the temple building was dimmed; with few resources and much opposition from foreigners living in the surrounding areas they stopped building and concentrated on the building of their own homes. They were struggling to survive for despite all their efforts they were experiencing very poor harvests, reaping barely enough to keep body and soul alive. It was at this point that the prophet Haggai spoke to them, a message from the Lord:

"You expected much, but see, it turned out to be little. What you brought home, I blew away. Why?" declares the LORD *Almighty "Because of my house, which remains a ruin, while each of you is busy with your own house. Therefore because of you the heavens have withheld their dew and the earth its crops." (Haggai 1:9-10)*

The governor Zerubbabel and the priest Joshua were convicted by this message as were all the people, so that they were obedient and returned to the building of the temple. As the building grew, the older people amongst them who had seen the former temple were very discouraged.

"Who of you is left who saw this house in its former glory? How does it look to you now? Does it not seem to you like nothing? But now be strong, O Zerubbabel", declares the Lord. "Be strong, Joshua son of Jozadak the high priest. Be strong all you people of the land", declares the Lord, "and work. For I am with you." (Haggai 2:3-4)

If they put all their best efforts into the building, God would supply the wealth to make this building even more glorious than the previous one.

There was another lesson that God had to teach them. Besides getting their priorities right, they also needed to be reminded that a holy God needed them to make a distinction between what is clean and what is defiled. God required clean or holy people to work on and in His Temple.

When through repentance they were cleansed, then God would bless them. This they were eager to put right. God loved them enough to persevere with them by sending a prophet to correct their wrong attitudes and ways. As ever the prophecy ends with a promise of the coming Messiah through the line of Zerubbabel who was himself a descendant of David.

Zechariah

Zechariah was a contemporary of Haggai and took over when Haggai ceased to prophesy. His prophecy was very different from that of Haggai. Most of it was given to him in the form of visions; vivid pictures which need interpretation, even for Zechariah. His is a far more complex book which has messages of hope and warnings for the people of that time but also warnings of God's plans for the near future and of the far distant future.

The latter has yet to be fulfilled.

God reminds the people of Jerusalem that He had had to punish their forefathers because although He had sent His prophets to warn them of their sinful ways, they gave no heed to such repeated warnings and continued to live as they wanted. Such a reminder from Zechariah was enough;

'Then they repented and said, "The LORD Almighty has done to us what our ways and practices deserve, just as He determined to do."(Zechariah 1:6)

God's promise to them for their return to Him was that He would take care of all nations who had shown nothing but cruelty toward them. Not only would He quell their enemies, but there would come a time when He would be with them.

"For I am coming, and I will live among you", declares the LORD. "Many nations will be joined with the LORD in that day and will become my people. I will live among you and you will know that the LORD Almighty has sent me to you." (Zechariah 2:10b-11)

This they understood as a promise of the Messiah, but did not grasp the fact that gentiles too would receive Him.

Zechariah

As a subject nation, they could not have the descendant of David, Zerubbabel, as a king, but God told Zechariah to make a crown for the high priest Joshua and anoint him. Such an appointment of a priest over his people would be acceptable to Persia.

There are throughout the book, many predictions of future events to warn the Israelites of future enemies whom the Lord will tackle for them, such as Greece.

> *"I will rouse your sons, Zion,*
> *against your sons, Greece,*
> *and make you like a warrior's sword."*
> *(Zechariah 9:13)*

God knew that His Word, the Bible would be read throughout the world, so that many of the warnings given by Zechariah of future events were indeed warnings to all nations concerning their relationship with the Jewish people. Many of these warnings were spoken of by Jesus and reiterated by His disciple John in the book of Revelation.

> *"This is the plague with which the Lord will strike all the nations that fought against Jerusalem their flesh will rot while they are still standing on their feet, their eyes will rot in their sockets, and their tongues will rot in their mouths. On that day men will be stricken by the Lord with great panic. They will seize each other by the hand and attack one another other. Judah too will fight at Jerusalem." (Zechariah 14:12-14)*

> *"Then the survivors from all the nations that have attacked Jerusalem will go up year after year to worship the King, the LORD Almighty, to celebrate the Feast of Tabernacles." (Zechariah 14:16)*

They will be punished if they do not go to celebrate.

Zechariah

Many who have access to this word, have had plenty of time to accept this warning and act upon it. There will be survivors in the guilty nations who will refuse to fight against the Jews and there will be a place for them in the kingdom which Jesus will set up.

Malachi

The prophecy of Malachi was given about one hundred years after the Jews returned from exile, several generations after Haggai and Zechariah spoke and caused the people to repent. However the prosperity of the land did not seem to be that much better. Their recent harvests had been poor and the frequent swarms of locusts made for a scarcity of food. The people were hungry and despairing.

They were attending the temple but half-heartedly; it had become a ritual which the sooner over, the better. The priests too had the same cavalier attitude toward worship and were conducting the services in a very careless manner.

Malachi was an anonymous prophet for the name given just means 'messenger' and was not a name given by the Jews to their children. His basic message to the people was that they had no right to blame God for their circumstances as they had started the break up in their relationship with God.

Malachi reminds them of all the love God has poured down upon them in the past, despite their wicked ways. If they were to consider the fate of other nations, especially Edom, they would realise how special they were to God. They must stop complaining for what they were lacking, and give thanks for what they had! They were to consider their own attitude toward God.

"'A son honours his father, and a servant his master. If I am a father, where is the honour due to Me? If I am a master, where is the respect due to Me?, says the Lord Almighty.

> "It is you, priests, who show contempt for my name. But you ask, 'How have we shown contempt for your name?"

Malachi

> *By offering defiled food on my altar.*
> *But you ask, 'How have we defiled you?" By saying that the LORD'S table is contemptible. When you offer blind animals for sacrifice, is that not wrong? When you sacrifice lame or diseased animals, is that not wrong?" (Malachi 1:6b-8b)*

The priests had also failed in that they were not teaching God's law but just telling the people what they wanted to hear.

The people were guilty of mixed marriages; finding partners in the surrounding nations. Nor were they true to their marriage partner but would dump an elderly wife for someone younger.

> *"The man who hates and divorces his wife," says the LORD, the God of Israel, "does violence to the one he should protect," says the LORD Almighty. So be on your guard, and do not be unfaithful.' (Malachi 2:16)*

Because they were God's people, they felt that God should be pleased with them, whatever they did.

Their ways are known by God, He mirrors their speech.

> *'(By saying,) "All who do evil are good in the eyes of the LORD, and he is pleased with them' or 'where is the God of justice?" (Malachi 2:17b)*

To which God promises to send another messenger in the future who would prepare the way for the Messiah. He would teach them how to live, and purify their lives. Another cause for God's anger was their unpaid tithes and offerings. The non-payment of these would bring a curse upon them as they were robbing God. A fact that they were very surprised to hear. If they would take the trouble to give God His due,

Malachi

*"Then all the nations will call you blessed, for yours will be a delightful land", says the L*ORD *Almighty.' (Malachi 3:12)*

Lastly He accuses them of slandering Him. God points out that they had said it was useless serving God because He never punishes evil doers so why not do as they do! God assures them, He is giving them time to repent but there would come a day when He would come as Judge and reward those who were righteous and punish the wicked.

*"Surely the day is coming; it will burn like a furnace. All the arrogant and every evildoer will be stubble and that day that is coming will set them on fire," says the L*ORD *Almighty.' (Malachi 4:1)*

Malachi states quite plainly that a loving God is merciful and very patient but in the end His love must be balanced with His justice for He is a holy God and must expect holiness from His people.

The loving Father who sends His Son to redeem mankind as recorded in the New Testament was also a God of Judgement.

The book of Revelation, the final book of the New Testament gives the account of the second coming of Jesus to bring victory to His followers but also to judge the whole world. It is not only in 'Revelation' that judgement is mentioned, it is also in the gospels as part of the message Jesus declares. We always have the choice, to follow Him or go our own way and suffer the consequences.